Red is the New Black

HOW WOMEN CAN FASHION
A MORE POWERFUL AMERICA

Cathy Lynn Taylor

A POST HILL PRESS BOOK

Red is the New Black:
How Women Can Fashion a More Powerful America
© 2016 by Cathy Lynn Taylor
All Rights Reserved

ISBN: 978-1-68261-196-8
ISBN (eBook): 978-1-68261-197-5

Cover Design by Jim DiMeo
Cover Photography by Lonna Sullivan
Capitol image by Shutterstock.com
Interior Design and Composition by Greg Johnson/Textbook Perfect

Post Hill Press
275 Madison Avenue, 14th Floor
New York, NY 10016
posthillpress.com

Printed in the United States of America

10 9 8 7 6 5 4 3 2 1

For J and C

Beloved #powergals

Contents

Preface

Over martinis, Manolos, and manicures, my friends and I chat about our jobs, relationships, real estate, and the latest *US Weekly* scandal. We are modern women living the *Sex and the City* dream—entrepreneurs, mothers, and fashion mavens who have managed to do it all. But there's one curious blind spot in my friends' worldview: they don't seem to be aware of how conservatism made all this possible.

As women today, we have a tremendous amount of power. Savvy women are taking over the world: More women than ever own businesses (29% of business owners and rising[1]), matriculate from medical or law school (47% of medical school matriculants[2], and 47.3% of law school matriculants[3]), and are the breadwinners of their households (a record 40% of households as of 2013[4]). We are living in a beautiful new dawn of women's achievement and empowerment, and women deserve to hear the substantive facts and arguments about the policies that shape our world. But when I started investigating the facts behind what really are the best public policies for women, I found the answers defied a lot of "common wisdom" about how women should vote. I knew I had to get the message out there, because it's more important than ever for public policy to shape this world in which women can lead our best lives.

For me, uncovering the true power of public policy in my life has been a lifelong journey. Long before I became openly political, I lived by a set of principles that I didn't label as liberal or conservative—I simply thought of them as common sense. But through an extraordinary combination of experiences on Wall Street, Main Street, and even Pennsylvania Avenue (the White House), I began to see the ways that public policy and my private ideals were firmly intertwined; at the same time, I saw how each of these "streets" could sometimes grow disconnected from others, and I realized the importance of educating people on how public policy touches us all.

I also realized that the ideals I'd simply thought of as common sense were actually a value system that defines my life and gives it meaning and purpose, from the boardroom to the family room. In particular, I identified seven core values that united my politics with my lifestyle and the ideas I hold closest to my heart—the seven values we'll explore together in this book. But, these are much more than simply my personal code; these are the principles that I believe unite all women, as well. For so many of us, we may not realize it but we already live by this code; now it is time for us to come together to support public policy that embodies it. To this end, I realized it was time for someone to lay out a substantive, data-driven examination of the policies that are closest to women's lives today, so that I could share the benefits that I've felt in my own life from my conservative worldview.

These core values: personal responsibility, financial independence, investment in opportunity, belief in the future, leadership by example, strength, and paying it forward, are all values that I shared with my hardworking friends on both sides of the aisle. Yet, the numbers prove that, as a female conservative, I'm an outlier. From the hipster college coed running an internet start-up to the 85-year-old Nanna who inquires weekly about her granddaughter's marriage prospects, far more American women identify themselves as Democrats than Republicans (52:35 of women lean Democratic, according to a July 2015 Pew study).[5] For decades, if a woman considered herself sympathetic to the poor, sensitive to the environment, and an advocate for peace over war, she likely considered herself a Democrat. No doubt, Democrats in the last few decades have been a lot better at talking to (and about) women. Conservatives have done poorly in listening to and connecting with women, and we have a bad track record of humoring public figures who don't represent the views of the bulk of conservatives when it comes to women and women's issues. This may explain why so many women live like conservatives, but identify as liberals. I would have been that way, too, if I hadn't taken my own unique path. But first, to understand what unites us, we have to understand what divided us in the first place.

Why can't we be friends?

The song "Why Can't We Be Friends?" is by a band called War. That's a little irony that could also be a metaphor for so much of the debate between liberals and conservatives.

We're all committed—liberal and conservative alike—to reducing suffering in the world. So why can't we get along?

The roots of the divide between liberalism and conservatism go way back. Conservatism is (confusingly enough) based on an Enlightenment-era school of thought called "classical liberalism." It was a big innovation in the concept of freedom as a God-given right that each individual is born with. Instead of treating individuals as pawns of the state, individual rights began to be explored in philosophy and politics as the end goal of policy-making. A lot of Enlightenment thinkers and leaders (including America's Founding Fathers) came to the conclusion that the best way to protect individual liberty is to minimize government intrusion into individual lives. The role of government, in their eyes, was to maintain the rule of law and provide a safe and fair environment in which people could pursue their own fates.

Modern liberalism sprang from a late nineteenth-, early twentieth-century school of thought called "progressivism." Progressivism sprang, in part, from an expanded interest in prag-matism, as politicians and philosophers weighed the concepts of "the greater good" versus individual liberty. They argued that sacrificing certain areas of individual liberty (by raising taxes or imposing greater government regulation) was worthwhile if it enhanced the overall quality of life for society, or the "greater good." They believed the government could serve to pro-actively improve lives through the distribution of benefits, jobs, services, and more; and that this process could also be used to eliminate social ills. This was a radical departure from the "classical liberal" view of government. Instead of limiting the government's primary role to the rule of law, progressives (and today's liberals) viewed government as a tool that could be used to enhance the lives of everyone through direct intervention.

In today's polarized political environment, it's easy to forget that we're all coming from the same place: trying to eliminate suffering and ensure fairness. Liberals have expressed fears about conservative ideas that appeal strongly to our appreciation of fair-ness and order: they say they don't want freedom to devolve into anarchy, and they don't want capitalism to devolve into a rat race in which people get left out in the cold. Liberals have also excelled at communicating with women on these issues, drawing on the sorts of real-life concerns that compassionate women care about deeply.

Liberals also claimed a monopoly on feminism in the 1960s and 70s, deepening the impression that the Democratic Party is inherently pro-woman and the Republican Party (by inverse) must be anti-woman.

So which ideology really offers women a better deal? My friends were skeptical so I decided what we need is a look at the facts.

It was a Republican President (Ronald Reagan) who appointed the first female Supreme Court Justice, Sandra Day O'Connor. It was a Republican President (George W. Bush) who will very likely go down in history for saving more female lives on earth through his President's Emergency Plan for Aids Relief (PEPFAR) than any world leader in history. And now, it is Republican women who are surging in the number of state legislature seats held, with 10% growth in the past year alone, while Democratic women in the same offices have stagnated or decreased.[6] This movement is significant because state legislature officials often move on to Congress and thus are considered an important indicator of the political sentiment in the country and the future composition of Congress. In other words, it is conservatives who will likely be sending more women to Washington. And, it was a Republican president who appointed me, a woman, to his National Security Council.

My hope is to illuminate how conservative policies really do make the world better for savvy women, but that doesn't mean I'm going easy on conservatives. Conservatives have let a few speak for many—and the wrong few, at that. Rogue, intermittent statements over the past two decades by the likes of Rush Limbaugh, who called student Sandra Fluke an unpleasant name, further fueled the liberal fire. Inadvertent comments by Presidential candidates that insinuate a lack of support for women's issues continue to do damage to the image of the Right Wing. Even when conservatism wins over some liberal women through good finance and security policies, too often when it comes to social issues, mixing women and conservatism has been like wearing polka dots with stripes.

I realized that if, as conservatives, we could learn to interact with women in a way that would encourage them to listen, they will find that conservatism offers them a more powerful set of beliefs by which to enhance their lives, as I've found in my own life. It's going to take a two-part process: calling out the people on the right who don't truly represent the majority's opinion on women and women's issues, and also putting our ideas out there in a manner that acknowledges the special challenges and decisions women face.

I was lucky that I got to learn from some great leaders, and that I had the opportunity to participate in a form of service to government that few have the privilege to experience. But in these times of crisis, conservatives can't rely on awakening one person at a time. The values I recognized as the core of conservatism are values that a lot of women are already living by. It's time to change the conversation—to stop the criticisms of the other side and to cease apologizing to women for conservatism's failures and missteps. Let's simply talk about which values are actually the best embodiment of women's power for good in the world…and for ourselves. How can we make public policy a better tool to enable and empower women? How can women use the principles we already live by in our private lives, in our public positions? I think the answers are in my new trend alert: *Red is the New Black.*

Chapter 1

Personal Accountability

You dart from your late-running meeting to the annual sample sale at your favorite shoe designer's boutique. You reach the store five minutes before they close, just in time to spot the one pair of positively purr-fect kitten heels you've been coveting for ages. As you reach for them, another woman pushes past you, knocking your latte onto your dress as she snatches the shoes without even a glance at you. What just happened?

Successful women live by a code of personal responsibility. We take accountability for our actions, and treat others as we wish to be treated. It's the foundation of who we are. But not everyone lives by our code. How did we come to this point at which, as women, we are united by the same aims (our gorgeous shoes!) but divided so deeply by our attitudes on how to attain them? A rude act in a shoe store may seem like an isolated incident, but sometimes it can be the sign of a cultural attitude of entitlement and irresponsibility gone too far.

When it comes to all public policy, the fundamental question that divides most of us is: how much government intervention do we want? But when it comes specifically to social policy, it is not only how involved we want the government to be, but also how involved *you*, each and every individual, want to be. The dividing line for social policy is whether you are willing to look after yourself to the fullest extent possible. This key question underlies every core social policy in America, from education to health care to abortion to civil liberties.

There's No "I" in Team but There is a "Me"

I've always found it a bit perplexing when someone says, "There's no 'I' in 'team,'" to admonish someone else for being self-centered. If you look closely, there *is* a "me" within the word "team." I like to reconcile the saying this way: there's no room on a team for one person's ego or self-focus, but because of our individuality and unique perspectives, each of us—you and me and we—are all a necessary and important part of any team. Together, we make a far more powerful team than any one of us alone.

The "me" in "team" has been a guiding principle of my day-to-day activities. Some of the most intimate aspects of my life are actually governed by our country's domestic policy—those laws and regulations that enable, guide, and even restrict our daily endeavors within America. These policies touch areas including education, health care, benefits such as welfare and social security, labor laws like minimum wage, and civil liberties that even affect what we're allowed to say and where. In other words, the choice of whether to take the path of personal responsibility is everywhere.

There was a time in my twenties, when I was working and living in New York, during which I realized how important my own sense of personal accountability would be to my core identity. My conservative awakening was a process that took finding a job, losing a job, being invited to work at the White House, and having a personal brush with the creation of life, to fully understand the value of personal accountability and how it had always been there, guiding my decisions. So why did it take so long for me to reach that conclusion?

Liberal Ladies and Conservative Curmudgeons

When it comes to social policy, liberalism seems like the kind-hearted way to go. It's not surprising that a lot of women are attracted to it like it's a tall, single guy with a steady job and his own place.

Liberals want what we all want: less suffering in the world. On its face, liberal policy says, "We don't want anyone to suffer. We want to cushion people from the consequences of their actions because everyone makes mistakes. We want to help people make the best decisions for them, and protect them from harm." This appeals strongly to us women because we're taught to be nurturers. Find me a woman who is raising her hand to say, "Yes, I'd like to see more suffering in the world, please!" Liberalism seems down-right lady-like.

Let's get this straight: *no one* wants to see more suffering in the world. Conservatives just have very different ideas of how to prevent suffering than liberals do. It doesn't help that many prominent conservatives—in the government and on the airwaves—focus more on the "bootstraps" part of their message than the compassionate side. Unfortunately, that makes it easy to paint conservatives as cold-hearted curmudgeons.

Today's highly polarized media environment can make it seem like choosing one approach or the other is a choice between good and evil, in which each side believes they are the One True Way. The reality is, there's a lot in common between what conservatives and liberals want, and holding either point of view doesn't automatically make you a fool or a bad person. There's a very old saying often attributed to Churchill, but actually predating him[1] (proving just how old this debate is!): "If you're not a liberal at age twenty-five, you have no heart. If you're not a conservative by age thirty-five, you have no brain."

At first glance, it seems conservatives come out on top in that statement, but it's a jab at both sides. The truth is, liberals are much better at communicating the "heart" of their message, while conservatives tend to focus on cold facts and grim statements of necessity. Just take a look at liberals' favorite conservative to hate, Wisconsin Governor Scott Walker. In supporting mandatory drug tests for welfare seekers, Walker infamously stated, "My belief is that we shouldn't be paying for them to sit on the couch, watching TV or playing Xbox."[2] We can debate the merits of mandatory drug testing for welfare recipients, but whatever your point of view is, it's undeniable that Walker's statement didn't do a good job of communicating conservative compassion toward the poverty-stricken or those struggling with addiction.

Walker's not alone in the foot-in-mouth department. In 2012, then-presidential candidate Mitt Romney was quoted saying, "I like being able to fire people." That's enough to make steam come out of nearly anyone's ears! But in context, Romney wasn't talking about taking pleasure in firing employees—he was talking about how much he valued the ability to change his health insurance plan if he wanted to ("firing" his insurer).[3] That's something lots of people would agree with, but the way Romney put it was a massive flop. It's enough to make conservatives groan, "Mitt, did you really have to say it like *that*?"

Think about the people in your life, though—people who represent a wide range of views. How many people could you say, with absolute certainty, want to see innocent, helpless, or disadvantaged people suffer? Just like Mitt Romney didn't actually mean he loves firing employees, many conservatives have good intentions behind their fumbling words—in fact, often they have the very same intentions that the majority of Americans have.

But when both sides retreat into their corners, it becomes impossible to find common ground. Liberals won't forgive conservatives' tone, effectively ignoring the substance of their remarks, while conservatives won't acknowledge the seriousness of their missteps, insisting that anyone with a brain should be able to see the wisdom of their points. Conservatives thus alienate anyone who might have qualms about conservatives' seeming lack of sympathy or compassion. It's no surprise that women flock to the liberal side.

Does Liberal = Kind + Compassionate?

No one wants to see families go without basic necessities, or society's most vulnerable left out in the cold. Whether we're dropping some canned goods off at our retired Nanna's place, or advising a friend to get out of a bad relationship, women are protectors and providers (despite anyone who might tell you those are men's jobs). That's why liberal policy is so appealing to many women: liberals claim the government is the best entity to protect and provide for all of society. But, unfortunately, it just so happens that the most efficient way for a big entity like government to "protect and provide" for hundreds of millions of people is to restrict their choices and funnel them all toward the single government vending machine of handouts.

So how does this tie back to the woman in the shoe store? The one who knocked your coffee over and snatched the shoes you wanted? It's not just that you lost the shoes. It's not just that you ruined your dress. It's the thought that people are willing to shove you aside to grab what they want. Politeness is more than a social nicety; it's a part of what hangs our society together—it's the outer face of personal accountability and respect toward others. As you can already tell, the problem goes *way* beyond sample sales.

So what's the difference between you and the woman who thought it was acceptable to bounce off you like a rubber wall to get to what she wanted? She was acting like a liberal and you were acting like a conservative.

I know. You immediately say aloud, "That doesn't sound very fair to liberals!" But, maybe the liberals you know are more conservative than you or any of them realize.

Choosing between conservative and liberal ideologies isn't a choice between good and evil, it's a choice between two methods of pursuing the same social benefits. The primary difference between conservative and liberal domestic or social policy is: conservatives try to ensure happiness and prosperity by creating equal ***opportunity*** for all. Liberals try to ensure happiness and prosperity by creating equal ***outcomes*** for all. That's where the traditional more government/less government divide between conservatives and liberals originates. To create more opportunity, conservatives often advocate for less government intrusion and restriction on individuals' lives, depending on the rule of law to help establish equal opportunities by creating a world in which government's main role is to keep people from defrauding each other, so they can compete fairly. This system depends heavily on personal accountability. Liberals tend to see government as an instrument of ensuring equal outcomes for individuals, however; they elect to remedy social maladies such as poverty by using the government's power to tax and regulate to redistribute wealth and services among all levels of society. However, after nearly a century of the political experiment of redistribution, when one in seven Americans live in poverty, our schools are failing, and it is easier to get an abortion than to think through your readiness for parenting, it is time to question government as the panacea to social ills. When people are sheltered from consequences, they also lose their sense of responsibility, and respect for themselves and the people around them.

In our shoe store example, you are respecting the rule of law and fair competition in order to get the shoes you want. Your opponent, on the other hand, may be acting out a conditioned response to an environment of handouts and entitlement: she who grabs the hardest and fastest gets the prize, and getting the prize is more important than responsibility for one's actions.

Many psychologists today are quantifying and studying what we always knew in our hearts: that children need to learn to take ownership of their actions in order to become successful, responsible, and empathetic adults.[4] Why wouldn't we have the same expectations for grown-ups? This is the real way to protect and provide for people, and reduce suffering overall: teach people to protect and provide for themselves. America needs domestic policies that serve and empower, underpinned by personal accountability.

President Ronald Reagan encountered significant criticism when he enacted policies to cut back government grants to nonprofits; one of his advisors, Michael Deaver, made matters worse when he told private charities to "pick up the slack."[5] That didn't paint an appealing picture—it made Reagan look like a cynical miser. At the time, nonprofits resented the move, blaming Reagan for tight competition over limited government grants.

However, Reagan didn't enact those policies because he wanted people to suffer. This is the same man who said, in his 1981 inaugural speech, "We shall reflect the compassion that is so much a part of your makeup. How can we love our country and not love our countrymen, and loving them, not reach out a hand when they fall, heal them when they are sick and provide opportunities to make them self-sufficient so they will be equal in fact and not just in theory?"[6]

Reagan's policies on nonprofits actually encouraged and enhanced charitable giving in practice: "In the Reagan years, charitable giving rose by more than 25 percent in inflation-adjusted dollars, twice the rate of the previous decade."[7] Donors did, indeed, step up.

Conservatives think that strong communities will take care of their most needy; that's why conservatives are such big supporters of private charity. Surprisingly, study after study demonstrates that conservatives give more to charity than liberals do![8] Conservatives understand that a local charity can be more accountable to results and efficiency than a massive government program run by unelected officials. And that's just a small piece of the big picture of how personal accountability drives conservative policy. So how would this all look in our shoe store?

If the sales associates were running the sample sale like a conservative government, everyone would be let in according to when they arrived to the store and would be free to seek the shoes they wanted—as long as they were available. But because your shoe nemesis's behavior was out of bounds (rushing in after you and knocking your coffee all over you), an attendant may step in and ensure the shoes are returned to you, thus enforcing the rule of law. And the presence of watchful associates, combined with a greater emphasis on personal responsibility, should discourage coffee-knocking in the first place.

If the sales associates were running the sample sale like a liberal government, they may ask both of you who is in greater need of the shoes, and then give them to the woman who makes a better case for her need, regardless of who got there first. The idea here is that coffee-knocking and other less-than-charming behavior should be discouraged because it's no longer necessary to resort to those tactics to get what you need; the associates will ensure each shopper receives what the associates deem she deserves...in theory.

How does this play out in real life? Three major areas of social policy provide great examples: welfare, abortion, and education.

Welfare Reform: "We Want to Prevent Suffering"

There's a hot debate in America at the moment regarding the notion of free stuff. Democratic candidates want to provide highly desirable benefits, like universal health care and college tuition. Republican candidates believe these benefits should be procured at a state and/or individual level. The Democratic point of view is that these benefits are basic rights that will help Americans prosper. The Republican viewpoint is that these benefits are important but must be valued, and thus invested in, by the individual, unless in the event of catastrophe, in which case the federal government can offer a safety net. The ideas of either side are not necessarily wrong; however, history has shown time and time again that benefits without a serious system of accountability have two failings: First, they are not sustainable as a cost to the taxpayer. Instead of solving a financial problem, they add regulation, complexity and expense, which compound the existing financial problem. Second, benefits that don't require recipients to "put some skin in the game" become less valued, less valuable, and more prone to fraud and exploitation, at a societal and economic cost.

"Welfare reform" is a phrase that gets tossed around a lot like a hot potato. Liberals use it like a bad word, while conservatives blink owlishly and say, "Well, who *doesn't* want to fix things?" It simply depends on who's doing the fixing. President Clinton's welfare reform bill of 1996 created the now all-too-familiar situation of workers who refuse to take on more hours because doing so endangers their benefits. The bill was enough to make one of his upper-level appointees, Peter Edelman, a confirmed Democrat, resign in protest, citing the bill as "the worst thing Bill Clinton has done."[9] This West Wing drama may seem miles away from your daily life, but it actually hits quite close to home. I experienced the consequences personally when my family sought elder care for my aging father-in-law in Vermont, and discovered it was extraordinarily difficult to find someone willing to work forty hours a week for us, because so many hourly workers didn't want to risk losing their low-income assistance benefits.

Conservative ideas for reform haven't gone over so well either, as described in the previous section. While conservatives have many sensible ideas about consolidating welfare programs and making them more effective, conservative tone-deafness when dealing with those in poverty led to an extremely odd incident in 2002 when protesters stormed The Heritage Foundation and threatened to pelt conservative welfare policy analyst Robert Rector with shoes.[10]

For the most part, however, conservatives tend to combine compassion with common sense. Contrary to what you might have heard, many conservatives (like me!) support a government safety net for those who face a major catastrophe. One good example of such a program is COBRA, the federal healthcare program that allows people who lose their jobs or encounter a life-changing event to continue their employer-provided healthcare coverage for up to eighteen months. However, reform is critically needed to ensure fraud is eliminated from our welfare system, programs are focused on getting people back on their feet (not sustaining them indefinitely), and recipients are required to demonstrate that they're contributing suitable efforts to minimize their time on welfare.

How have liberal policies fared by these standards? According to one analyst, Clinton's 1996 welfare reform "may have initially reduced poverty, [but] it left those still living at that income level worse off than they were before, reaching fewer of them and giving those it did reach less."[11] While overall poverty levels were reduced during Clinton's era, his reforms also seemed to generate "a huge spike in *extreme* poverty."[12] In other words, those who remained poor were getting poorer...much poorer. Another drawback of Clinton's reforms developed as time wore on and the economy began to take another downturn; those who really needed the assistance most didn't seem to be getting it. Now welfare was both expensive *and* ineffective. Where was all this money going? Well, part of the problem seems to be that when money was allocated to states in a lump sum with relatively little accountability for this program, it was often portioned off into other programs that didn't as directly, or effectively, assist the poor.[13] So no one along this money train—the states receiving the block grants or the individuals receiving benefits—had the "skin in the game" to ensure their participation was focused toward individual and economic improvement.

Liberal welfare policy hasn't been exactly great for women, in particular. President Ronald Reagan once said, "The best social program is a productive job for anyone who's willing to work."[14] But liberal policies in the last eight years have had the opposite effect, destroying jobs…with a disproportionate effect on women. From 2009 through March 2012, men lost 57,000 jobs, but women lost 683,000 jobs.[15] Two million women have fallen into poverty in that time—that's more than 16 percent of women.[16] Even in their personal sphere, it seems liberal politicians aren't working toward women's prosperity: President Obama's White House paid female employees 13 percent less than what male employees earned,[17] while Hillary Clinton paid female staffers about three quarters the amount she paid male staffers, according to Senate budget data.[18] Yet, liberals claim they want to advance the economic interests of women. In fact, under liberal policies, while men's wages have made slight improvements in the last four years as America struggles out of recession, women's wages have continued to decline.[19] The situation is especially dire for single mothers, whose poverty rate is nearly twice that of single fathers.[20] Yet this was during an era in which liberal economic policies reigned, with the supposed goal of lifting everyone—including women—out of poverty.

I graduated college in a terrible job market during the early 90s, when Clinton's policies were just going into effect. Like many graduates today, my first prospects in the job market were bleak—and they got even bleaker when my very first job fell through, leaving me unemployed, inexperienced, and under-qualified in New York City. At the urging of friends, I signed up for unemployment benefits. I can safely say it was one of the most demoralizing experiences of my life. My self-esteem plummeted and, instead of finding comfort and security in the assistance, I only felt drearier about my future. After a few short months, I chose to work for a temp agency (even though it would mean sacrificing my benefits without any clear promise of steady income) rather than remain on unemployment. Six years and an MBA later, I returned to one of the companies for which I'd worked as a temp, this time working as a highly trained mortgage bond trader. I know how it feels to need help and I remembered that feeling as I approached my role as a financial policy advisor in the White House.

My time at the White House was a wakeup call. I'd volunteered for various organizations my whole life, and thought I'd known what it meant to sacrifice for others, but then I met the people who'd dedicated their lives and careers to making America— and the world—better. They taught me what the true definition of service was. They worked hard, often with very little obvious reward, but as soon as I experienced the fulfillment of seeing my ideas and policy recommendations improve the lives of others, I realized why. That experience crystallized for me what I had been beginning to become aware of since graduating college—that helping others and personal responsibility went hand in hand.

To fully understand welfare and how to fix it, let's go back to the beginning and take a look at how it all began.

Welfare as we know it today began with The New Deal, a series of policies and programs set in place by President Franklin D. Roosevelt in the depths of the Great Depression. When America faced unprecedented suffering and poverty, Roosevelt believed the best and most effective way to protect those who fell victim to hard times was through massive government intervention. This included subsidizing certain activities (like agriculture), funding work programs, and creating other programs and agencies to distribute financial aid directly to families.

Subsequent generations grew up taking it for granted that the government's role in their lives included providing a safety net if they fell on hard times. The innovations of The New Deal opened up the possibility of creating other familiar forms of government assistance. Today, millions of people depend, to some degree, on government assistance to meet their daily needs (52.2 million, 20% of the American population—or, one in five people).[21] You probably have friends who benefit from policies originated in The New Deal, and you might not even realize it.[22]

Conservatives' main objection to New Deal-inspired policies is that they are often followed by massive instances of fraud and corruption, demonstrate few measurable results, and damage economic prosperity in a way that keeps *everyone* down. And underpinning the economic reasons for welfare reform is a philosophical reason: fostering a culture of dependence and entitlement is not only unsustainable—as it undermines America's growth and prosperity—but it also deprives citizens of the personal fulfillment of achieving one's own success. When one in five Americans receives government benefits in some form or another, it seems like these programs are no longer just about helping the poorest of the poor or those who have suffered recent catastrophe; they start to look like the status quo.

Today's welfare policy challenges are considerable: the policies require an income redistribution that is fundamentally un-American, they are fraught with fraud and irresponsible expense, and they incent reliance rather than independence.

Consider 2004, in which a total of $1 trillion was transferred from the pockets of the top two quintiles of American earners, and funneled into services primarily benefiting the bottom three quintiles.[23] This is a massive reallocation of income into programs that aren't doing much to help people get back on their own two feet—and are, in fact, harming institutions like marriage that could provide the stability for these receivers of benefits to go off the dole.[24]

Government spending on welfare rose 32%, to a high of $1 trillion,[25] under the most recent liberal presidency. However, according to a recent Government Accountability Office (GOA) report, "improper payments" (wasteful spending due to error or fraud) of welfare benefits rose to nearly $125 billion in 2014.[26] This is more than just a big chunk of money; it's a big chunk of government. The wasteful spending was traced to 124 programs across 22 agencies. The problem is systemic.

And that's just the money that's being improperly disbursed to claimants who are actually dead (much of that money is being reeled in by fraudsters using the deceased's personal information to claim their government assistance). What about the money that actually makes it to the people who qualify for it? Is it helping them get back on their feet?

To start, we can ask if welfare is encouraging people to give up the bad behaviors that might have landed them in hard times in the first place. Several states have tried to pass legislation that would require welfare applicants to pass a drug test before receiving benefits—as Florida Governor Rick Scott put it, if you apply for a job, you often have to pass a drug test to qualify for employment, so why not do the same to qualify for welfare benefits, which are often supposed to be a temporary measure to help someone out while they attempt to reenter the job market?[27] The Florida drug testing law was struck down in court, causing many other states to abandon their efforts to pass similar legislation, out of fear of litigation. Many liberals hailed this outcome as a triumph, even though 71% of Floridians supported the drug testing law.[28]

Getting clean and sober should be one of the fundamental ways that a person demonstrates they're ready to start rebuilding their life and independence. And they're not alone in the struggle to get clean—the government also funds plenty of programs to assist those struggling with addiction,[29] including millions of dollars in block grants to substance abuse prevention and treatment services,[30] alongside the many private charities that serve addicted populations. Conservatives aren't trying to leave anyone out in the cold. But conservatives do want to ensure that people who receive government assistance are as committed to getting on their own two feet again as the government is to helping them.

Just in case you needed more proof that welfare in its current form *isn't* about getting back on your feet, let's explore the widespread phenomenon of underemployment *encouraged* by welfare. The Congressional Budget Office (CBO) estimates that the equivalent of about 2.5 million full-time workers will leave the workforce by 2024 due to employment disincentives from the Affordable Care Act (ACA, also known as Obamacare) alone.[31]

Maybe you know someone whose nanny or housecleaner declined more hours because it would disqualify her for welfare benefits. Or maybe you know a recent college graduate struggling to launch her career, who turned down a part-time job offer because it threatened her unemployment check. These decisions are a result of what is often called the "welfare cliff."

That sounds scary – you don't want to imagine people in need falling off a cliff when they seek help! But the important part to realize is that this is a cliff created by welfare itself, not by poverty. That same CBO report on the economic effects of the ACA states, "CBO estimates that the ACA will reduce the total number of hours worked, on net, by about 1.5 percent to 2.0 percent during the period from 2017 to 2024, almost entirely because workers will choose to supply less labor—given the new taxes and other incentives they will face and the financial benefits some will receive." Additionally, "Although CBO projects that total employment (and compensation) will increase over the coming decade, that increase will be smaller than it would have been in the absence of the ACA. The decline in fulltime-equivalent employment stemming from the ACA will consist of some people not being employed at all and other people working fewer hours[.]"[32]

In other words, people aren't just going on welfare because it's more lucrative than getting a job; they're also losing jobs because welfare raises taxes so high that employers can't afford to take on more workers, and the entire economy struggles. And these are just the projected results of *one* program.

Welfare cliffs aren't new, though. They've been around for a while, and their cause can be found in several liberal policies. According to a paper by Senate Budget Committee Ranking Member Jeff Sessions, "Federal policy seeks expanded welfare enrollment as an explicit goal—regardless of need."[33] When your goal is to serve the most people, instead of the most needy, you wind up creating incentives to receive benefits instead of working. On top of that, according to Sessions, "Eligibility standards have been loosened as benefits have increased."[34] In other words, it's becoming easier *and* more lucrative to depend on government assistance.

Welfare can have a negative impact on women's lives in particular, as well. Welfare has been linked to lower marriage rates among the poor, as women seek to preserve the higher government benefits that come with single status.[35] Yet single parenting is a major risk factor for poverty and can ensure that a woman, and her children, remain poor.

Conservatives don't want to punish the poor. We're not the Scrooges the media makes us out to be. But we want to help the country's poverty-stricken two ways: by helping them get back on their feet, *and* by creating an economy in which they can thrive, and in which their eventual success isn't punished with redistributive policies.

Let's redefine welfare to what it was originally intended to be: temporary assistance for a small group of the nation's most impoverished families, designed to guide them back to self-sufficiency. Welfare reform should focus on results-based programs, in order to ensure those who need help truly receive it, and that such help propels them toward independence and success. Fraud needs to be eliminated, and standards need to be set in place to ensure that those who are applying for programs such as unemployment benefits are sincerely looking for work. Money should be funneled into job-readiness programs and other programs that actively assist recipients in getting on their own two feet.

Abortion: "Everyone Makes Mistakes"

Another aspect of liberal policy that appeals to our feminine side is forgiveness: everyone makes mistakes, so let's try to cushion people from the consequences of their actions.

I believe that when a woman has sex, she makes a choice about the risks she exposes herself to. One of those risks is pregnancy. While I may be an abortion moderate by conservative standards, supporting exceptions to some abortion restrictions in the case of rape or incest, I believe that providing free, government-backed abortions is a bad idea, morally and economically. Legalizing abortion may not reduce unwanted pregnancy as much as simply expanding access to contraceptives, according to data from some countries.[36] Look at it this way: educating women on the consequences of their choices, and how to prevent those consequences, will do a better job of reducing unfavorable outcomes than shielding women from those consequences.

When other women find out that I'm pro-life, many of them inevitably say, "Women should be in charge of their own bodies," or, "How can you let the government decide what you should be able to do with your body?" And, frankly, I couldn't agree more! But here's the thing: being pro-life isn't being anti-choice. I *am* afforded a choice. I'm just making that choice when I actually have the sex instead of once I discover I may be pregnant. Why is it any less of an empowering choice to protect myself when I have sex than it is to consider terminating a pregnancy?

I do believe in considerations for mothers' lives and in the case of rape and incest. I also support partial term limits as a path toward getting to a place in which everyone accepts personal accountability for their actions. But I stand against the policy of offering elective abortion, at nearly any point during pregnancy, as a widespread and acceptable form of family planning.

My views are based on the values necessary for a society in which life is respected at any age, and from a deeply personal experience. Single and over 35, I worried endlessly that I might never have the opportunity to have children. I took faith in the possibility that I could bear or adopt a child on my own at some point in the future. I also just had a lot of faith in God. I had been in a relationship with my now-husband since age 34. We both firmly believed in waiting to have children until we could responsibly provide for them, monetarily and as a nurturing family unit. I was ready to make that commitment to him earlier than he was, for he was free from the nagging of that darn biological clock. Finally, at age 39, I found myself a newlywed and ready to start a family. We tried for a few months and I proactively involved an expert OB/GYN specializing in AMA, which I had previously only known to stand for "American Medical Association," but apparently also means "Advanced Maternal Age," an acronym that is as common, in urban areas like New York City, as "LOL!"

Unfortunately, the statistics for AMA conception are not so pretty, so the doctors weren't particularly optimistic that I would be able to conceive naturally, and recommended I soon begin in vitro fertilization (IVF). I had mixed feelings about IVF, but I desperately wanted a child, so I underwent the counseling and training. As I left the training session and hopped into a cab to the airport for a short getaway with my husband, I broke down in tears. This was complicated stuff—how had so many of my dear friends undergone this scary process multiples times on their own and without complaint, giving themselves shots of potent chemicals at home and enduring many other ordeals? How would I do this? I prayed. I prayed I would not have to do this. Sometime around that weekend, unbeknownst to us, my prayers were answered and we conceived our first daughter.

Weeks later, knowingly pregnant but early enough that implantation wasn't guaranteed, I was receiving one of the weekly acupuncture treatments I had started a few months earlier, along with eating lots of high protein, high fat foods like avocados and walnuts (maybe old wives tales, but it couldn't hurt, right?). My close friend, "A," had undergone two IVF cycles like a champ and ultimately gave birth to amazing twins. She swore by the acupuncture and shared with me that she liked to use the quiet time to think about the type of mother she hoped to be. I loved that advice and so, lying there covered in needles, in the warm, new-agey fourth floor walk-up acupuncture office with the hum of NYC traffic below, I prayed again. During that prayer, I made a bit of a deal with that little pre-implanted peanut in my tummy, all but begging her to stick, to be strong during pregnancy. And, all of a sudden, as I lay there, a force, a tremor so significant that it's impossible to replicate or explain, rattled within my entire stomach area. It was almost alien-like, to be honest. But, then, I knew. Our Peanut had heard me. Peanut was there.

I never took a yoga class until my late 30s. I barely know my zodiac sign and, admittedly, couldn't tell you the signs of my children. I had never considered myself a particularly spiritual person beyond practicing my religion. But that incident in the acupuncturist's office gave me a new meaning for when and what life in my belly meant. For all intents and purposes, I became a mother that evening and I would never be the same again, no matter what would transpire during my pregnancy.

There have been more than 1 billion abortions worldwide since 1980. Developing nations have a much higher rate of abortion, as you would expect. But even in developed nations, 28% of pregnancies end in abortion.[37]

In the US, abortions peaked in the early eighties and now remain steady at about 1 million per year. More than half of the states have passed "right to know" legislation, which ensures women know the risks, realities, and alternatives related to abortion before they can terminate a pregnancy. Other efforts to offer alternatives including waiting periods, limits on taxpayer funding, laws requiring ultrasound viewing, partial term laws, and other mitigation efforts.[38]

Abortion goes to the core of my conservative views, so much so that I take an almost libertarian approach: my gut instinct is that the government should not tell women, or anyone else for that matter, what to do with our bodies. If states want to make laws discouraging abortion, people can make a choice about which state they want to live in. That's the idealistic stance, but, in reality, the problem with unregulated abortion is twofold: First of all, more than ever, we want and need a society in which all lives matter, so we must do a better job ensuring all lives are respected, even if there's an argument about the exact day or month at which that life begins. Secondly, abortions are symptomatic of a problem with poverty and lack of resources that is growing rather than diminishing in our country. Abortions are sought more by single, young, lower income, black women than by any other female group. In the US, nearly 25% of all pregnancies end in induced abortion. The bulk of these abortions are sought by young women in their teens and twenties, and two thirds of these are by unmarried women. Lower income women are more likely to have abortions and black women are three times more likely to end a pregnancy.[39] Also concerning, half of all pregnancies in the US are unintended. How, as women, can we find ourselves in the position that half of our pregnancies are unintended? That's not the government's fault. If we want to take control of our lives as women, the most powerful point at which we can do it is when we make choices about when and how to have sex.

These stats reveal that abortion is treating the symptom, not the cause, of a social problem.

When women are held responsible for their choices, they're more likely to make responsible choices. But either way, the terms pro-choice and pro-life are misnomers. Women are making a choice when we engage in sexual relations. We need to consider the consequences at the time of that choice, to avoid having to make a far more difficult and consequential choice later. We don't need more handouts; we need a society that promotes individual responsibility and awareness. Unwed childbearing has risen steadily in the U.S. despite the availability of legal abortion, and 37% of single-parent households lack self-sufficiency.[40]

A key aspect of solving many of these issues as they impact us in our day-to-day lives is a new definition and manifestation of family planning—organizations that help people consider and prepare for pregnancy far beyond contraception. This means going beyond just offering abortive or contraceptive services, to helping people consider budgets, childcare, marital support, and eldercare stress management, as well as offering a value system that will sustain them and their families. Families—and especially mothers—are in need of help and support more than ever as religious institutions play less of a role in communities (according to recent Pew research, the number of Christians in America has declined as those unaffiliated with any faith has risen),[41] globalization enables family members to disperse to follow their dreams around the world, and the demands on parents and families increase. How can we offer the support they need, and where can it come from? America needs to figure that out and create better family support and planning layer of civil society. Let's start by inventing more vigorous programs aimed at planning and support throughout pregnancy and beyond, robust family planning education, and a remedy to the welfare programs that incentivize single motherhood over the nuclear families that best benefit children *and* parents.

Education: "Help Them Make the Best Decisions"

There are few, if any, who would disagree that the U.S. education system is badly in need of a mom takeover. By almost every measure, our schools are failing our children and our families. At their creation, public schools sounded like a good idea: schools funded by tax money, meeting high standards of achievement, and ensuring that every child enters civic life with a basic understanding of how the world, and America's government, works. After all, that's why Thomas Jefferson supported public education: because a republic works best if the voting public is educated and informed. In a famous letter to George Wythe in 1786, Jefferson wrote, "I think by far the most important bill in our whole code is that for the diffusion of knowledge among the people. No other sure foundation can be devised, for the preservation of freedom and happiness."[42]

What it is likely Jefferson *didn't* envision was a public education machine that forces most parents to hunt for the least bad school to send their children to, instead of affording them the freedom to choose the *best*.

Today, more than one half of public school students in America are in poverty.[43] Yet, because of the monopoly of public schools on education funds, these students are forced to attend schools that will likely do little to lift them out of poverty. According to research by the Council on Foreign Relations, the United States invests more in public education than most other developed countries, but our students don't even rank in the top 10 in reading, science or math compared to other developed nations. More than 25 percent of U.S. students do not graduate high school in four years; for Hispanic and African-American students, the number nears 40 percent. Furthermore, an estimated 30 percent of high school graduates lack the basic math, science, and reading skills to pass the necessary tests required to enter the military.[44] Yet, without access to vouchers, charter schools, or other options, our most impoverished children have no choice but to attend the worst schools in the country, ensuring the cycle of poverty continues.

That reveals the problematic side of the liberal mission of "saving people from themselves" by putting them on a narrow path: restricting choices gives more control to the government, and control is addictive. It's an attitude that bleeds out into more areas than just education policy.

If public education is to get back on track, standards are key—even if you are completely libertarian, I think we can all agree that as a nation we need to ensure a certain level of access, competency, and progress in our school system.

But who sets those standards? Federal oversight of education began in 1965 with the Elementary and Secondary Education Act (ESEA), signed into law by President Lyndon Johnson, a former teacher himself, who believed that educational opportunity should be "our first national goal."[45] It would be decades before another president enacted substantive education policy reform—decades in which American schools steadily declined.

The education problem is a tough nut to crack. Task force after task force of the country's greatest minds have tried to tackle it. Ronald Reagan himself attended fifty-one meetings just to discuss the results of the groundbreaking report, *A Nation at Risk*.[46]

One of America's most heralded CEOs, Lou Gerstner, who oversaw IBM Corporation during tremendous growth and expansion, has devoted his post-business career to education reform. In 2008, he wrote, "High school and college graduation rates, test scores, and the number of graduates majoring in science and engineering are all flat or down over the past two decades."[47] And our students' performance is poorer than that of other nations during this time. What happened over the last twenty years to cause these declining standards?

Speak to most experts and they'll tell you a big part of the problem is teacher preparedness. Guaranteed tenure is partly to blame. Historically, a widely recognized problem with communism is that a guaranteed job provided no motivation to rise or improve performance, yet our public schools are ruled by a system in which tenured teachers are virtually guaranteed a job for life no matter what they do, good or bad.

Think about this: In New York City, roughly 200 teachers sit in empty rooms collecting full pay (costing taxpayers $22 million) because it's next to impossible to fire them.[48] You can thank teachers unions for this innovation of the public school system, called "rubber rooms."

Teachers unions got started on a solid principle: protect teachers from exploitation and abuse by unscrupulous employers. Unfortunately, the ills caused by teachers unions have become greater than those they were designed to protect against. Union rules and tenure make it so difficult to fire teachers who under-perform (or even, in some cases, those under investigation for molesting students) that in some places, like New York City, those teachers are simply assigned to an empty room where they sit all day, collecting full pay.

Our tax money funds public schools, whether we want it to or not—whether we even send our kids to the local public school or not. Why can't that money flow in a more productive direction? School districts across the country are trying to implement school choice programs that use taxpayer funds to sponsor scholarships to the schools of parents' choice, and other free market reforms; but those efforts are facing serious opposition from teachers unions and other liberal groups.[49]

That's because teachers unions aren't about teachers anymore. In fact, teachers unions oppose some free-market education reforms that stand to benefit teachers enormously, such as merit pay and alternative certification. Teachers unions have grown so big, and have gained such powerful allies, that they have become a cause in and of themselves, independent of education. Their cause isn't supporting better education for all; it's about keeping teachers unions in control, and that hurts students, parents, *and* average working teachers, too. Many teachers disagree with their unions' policies or even wish to opt out of membership in their union, but membership is a requirement of employment at public schools and mandatory membership fees can range up to $850 per year, leading some teachers to fight the rule of the unions in court.[50]

Another enormous obstacle to academic achievement facing lower economic students is a lack of stable home life, including insufficient food and nutrition. Without a safe home in which to study or the right diet to feed their minds, America's most vulnerable students are set up to fail. These are issues we can address in our approach to family planning and welfare described in the previous sections.

It's amazing to think that despite all this turmoil and the ominous data we received about school performance, it was not until almost forty years after the initial passage of the ESEA that education reform got successfully revisited, as it did under George W. Bush with No Child Left Behind (NCLB).

Despite liberal's criticism of NCLB, liberals had a long, long time to do something about education, yet the call for reform went unanswered prior to NCLB. Interestingly, NCLB was actually a more liberal than conservative approach in many ways. Traditionally, conservatives want to move control away from the federal government and into the hands of the states, but in this case, "Papa W" took a tough love approach and essentially said to the states, "You've been failing this education thing and making a mess of your budgets, so we're taking over to ensure everyone has access, standards, and results." This conservative reform had a powerful impact on women, in particular. In 2000, the female dropout rate from high school was 10 percent. By 2013, it halved to 6 percent. However, from 1990-2000, (before NCLB) progress in reducing the female dropout rate was much slower.[51]

As you can imagine, many conservatives were not happy about the large role of the federal government in education thanks to NCLB. But after federal education policy was virtually ignored for forty years, while standards and results slipped, many of us were glad to see someone stand up and be the parent in the proverbial classroom. What's transpired is that the weak schools with potential boned up and got better. The really weak ones have crumbled, and while that's a shame for both the schools and the students, it is better we deal with that and get these students into the right learning environment than let poor schools fester. Now that the education system has undergone what is similar to a market correction, a bipartisan congressional effort produced the Every Student Succeeds Act, which President Obama signed into law in 2015, returning power back to the states. However, whether the improvements attained under NCLB will sustain in the absence of its oversight and accountability measures remains to be seen. Elements of NCLB that were critical to shifting the pendulum on education's fate, like consequences for poor performers, are watered down to now include only the bottom 5 percent.[52]

So what are the components of successful school reform? The ingredients are simple, but the recipe is complex: teacher quality and training; choice, including vouchers and charter schools; and common standards combined with performance measurement.

Perhaps one of the most valuable imports America could make in the next few years is an importation of values and commitment from Singapore. According to recent data, "Since 2000, Singapore's students have been consistently high performers on international assessments…. In the 1990s, the Ministry of Education developed a comprehensive plan to attract high-quality people into education and support them in their work. Over time, a series of steps were taken, including recruiting teachers form the top one-third of academic performers… strengthening teacher training…and, very importantly, systematically developing career paths that enable teachers to build their skills and responsibilities over time."[53]

America has a lot of catching up to do in the realm of teacher training. In 2013, a report from the National Council on Teacher Quality found that "the bar is set too low for entrance into professional training, future teachers are not being adequately prepared for the classroom or new requirements such as the Common Core State Standards, and the nation's expectations are far below those for teachers in countries where their students score higher on international exams."[54] This wasn't news to Arthur Levine, president of the Woodrow Wilson Foundation, who found similar results in a 2006 study.[55]

There is hope, however. Independent organizations such as Teach for America are taking matters into their own hands by training and placing highly qualified teachers in underserved schools. According to the TFA website, "Between 2009 and 2013, statewide studies in North Carolina, Tennessee, and Louisiana concluded that TFA is among each state's top teacher-preparation programs."[56]

In addition to encouraging better training programs, we must break the stranglehold of teachers unions on the quality standards for hiring at public schools. These unions have blocked valuable reforms, such as merit-based pay for teachers, which have the potential to attract and retain high-quality teachers to public schools. Liberals will say states with more collective bargaining power have high per student funding and other positive metrics,[57] but other studies show there's really no correlation.[58] And if it were true that teachers unions achieve higher pay and there is, in turn, some correlation between higher teacher pay and student performance, then that's just more reason to pay the best teachers more money—why would the unions argue against that?

As we've discussed, teachers' unions, which began with the noble aim of protecting teachers from exploitation, have become one of American education's biggest obstacles. Another way to circumvent the unions, and give students access to a wider range of potentially higher-quality teachers, is to encourage school choice.

School choice encompasses a variety of programs united by the core idea that families should be able to choose where to spend their education dollars. School choice includes voucher programs, which give parents and students the opportunity to apply a tax-funded voucher to tuition at a private school of their choice; charter schools, which are free, openly-enrolled, public-ly-funded schools that operate independently of teachers' unions; and programs to fund and encourage online education.

A more free-market–education world not only allows parents to make the choices that are best for their families, but also sets an example for the next generation, through teachers who are held to a high bar of personal accountability for their work. School choice has been proven to raise student achievement, even at public schools, which must now up their game to compete with other area schools.[59] A 2014 study found that charter schools had 7 to 11% higher graduation rates than their public school counter-parts,[60] and in New York, vouchers to private schools increased the likelihood that participating black students would attend college by 24 percent.[61] Accountability and choice work!

But, heartbreakingly, many of America's neediest families get a taste of opportunity only to have it snatched away by school choice's political foes, and the vagaries of budget-making. In Connecticut, parents are fighting to maintain funding for charter schools,[62] while in Washington, DC, the successful DC Opportunity Scholarship Program was allowed to expire in 2009 due to political pressure, despite raising the graduation rate of participating students,[63] and was only reintroduced after two years of struggle.

School choice is often overlooked on the national stage, as it is often considered a local issue, but past support from major national figures has helped to bolster local communities against the continual onslaught of objections from special interest groups with job preservation as their primary aim. Just as we did with NCLB, conservatives must not let the perfect be the enemy of the good when seeking to limit federal involvement in local education decisions. A strong federal stance in favor of school choice could change not just our academic outcomes, but also the lifelong economic outcomes that result from better education.

It's hard to believe, but there is actually one issue that liberal teachers' unions and some ultra-conservative groups agree on: they abhor national standardized testing. Teachers unions object to the use of student achievement as a metric of teacher success (go figure), while conservatives bristle at the federal intrusion into local education.

I have to ruffle both their feathers a little bit by pointing out that accountability works; the problem is the standards and tests we're using. As with every issue in this chapter, programs must have measurable criteria of success in order to ensure effective operation. These metrics don't just help us understand *how* a program performs; they create a powerful incentive for program administrators to run their programs well before anyone even looks into them. Accountability is a powerful thing. And there's a compromise coming that should satisfy both sides, if we could all put our sharpened quills down and listen.

Hopefully, the Every Student Succeeds Act achieves the optimal balance of retaining the necessary standards-based performance measuring of the original law while handing much more of the standard-setting power back to states and local control. According to Jeanne Allen, founder of the Center for Education

Reform, "The Student Success Act [sic] swings the pendulum back to minimal federal intrusion in state affairs. It restores to the states power to implement current federal programs, gives local school districts more leeway on accountability and testing, ensures that reporting and accountability for federal funds are transparent, and provides incentives for states and schools that offer choices to parents. The bill provides flexibility and autonomy in developing rigorous state standards and meaningful school-choice programs."[64]

I went to a top public school. I was reasonably smart, and got to college through hard work; I studied for hours every night, played multiple varsity sports, was editor of the school newspaper, and participated in a variety of volunteer activities. But when I got to Duke, I almost flunked out in my first semester. I discovered that despite what I had thought was a great high school education, I hadn't learned how to write, how to do math, or, most importantly, how to learn. Fortunately, I had strong family nucleus and good examples from the students around me, and I figured it out. But it wasn't until graduate school that I finally learned how to learn, acquiring the critical thinking and studying skills necessary to grow and improve myself in school *and* beyond. I was lucky in my journey because I had stability and access to resources that many in America don't. But for many disadvantaged students, school is all they have, and if they don't receive the education they need there, they'll be doomed to repeat the cycle of poverty. If we're to support any of the reforms explored earlier in this chapter, which promote self-sufficiency and financial independence, we must in good conscience create an educational environment in which everyone has an equal opportunity to access the best possible education and succeed.

Conservative Darcy, Liberal Wickham

Let's go back to the sample sale from the beginning of this chapter. You're standing there, staring aghast at your ruined dress while your shoe-shopping rival has long ago headed to the cash register, not a care in the world. What does this have to do with social safety nets or personal freedom, anyway?

It boils down to this, a truth that we'll explore throughout this book: government policies are about more than boring speeches on CSPAN and numbers in a column on your tax forms. Public policy is a statement of how we choose to organize ourselves as a society: the kind of life we want to live and the kind of people we want to be.

Liberal policies are a bit like Mr. Wickham from *Pride and Prejudice*. He was portrayed as the philandering boss, Daniel Cleaver (Hugh Grant), in the *Pride and Prejudice* retelling, *Bridget Jones's Diary*. Cleaver and the original Wickham are charmers. They know how to flatter and they can make some genuinely nice gestures—think of the romantic weekend getaway Cleaver takes Bridget on in the movie. Cleaver and Wickham aren't *evil* characters. They just lack personal responsibility, and it takes a crisis for the heroine to see that darker side of him.

Mr. Darcy, on the other hand, might come across as cold and forbidding at first, but, once you crack the surface, you discover his genuine kindness (looking after his little sister, and being a good steward of the needs of the village neighboring his estate) and true wisdom (in his ability to ward off the attentions of the superficial Miss Bingley). In *Bridget Jones's Diary*, he's a good son, an attentive and caring suitor to Bridget on her birthday, and a hardworking and respected barrister.

A world in which people take responsibility for their actions is a world in which everyone is a bit more thoughtful and considerate toward each other, whether it's in their personal life, at the sample sale, or in City Hall and Washington, DC.

Value One: Personal Accountability

Darcy and Wickham/Cleaver are *living* conservative and liberal principles. One has a strong sense of personal accountability, and the other doesn't. And personal accountability isn't just a "guy thing," either. Women need it just as much as men.

As women, we need to be personally accountable not only to enhance our own strength, but also because it has historically led to better policies for our country. President George W. Bush may not be a media darling, but he did, at great political cost, enact the first sweeping education reform in more than forty years. It wasn't perfect and it has needed subsequent refinement, but at least he saw an area of our society in distress and took action. Democratic Presidents have had full congressional control eight times in their twenty total years in office since 1975, but not one of them thought, "Hmmm, we are lagging behind at least twelve other countries in literacy, numeracy, and problem solving…maybe we should do something about that."

Personal accountability doesn't just lead to better policies. It also leads to better governance and better personal interactions.

Consider this letter recently written to *New York Times Magazine*'s "Ethicist,"[65] a "Dear Abby" of sorts: "Close friends of mine are raising four young children in a city with an extremely high cost of living. Not a small feat. They are not millionaires, but they are not poor either. Because of the school zone in which they live, they prefer to send their children to a private school, where tuition is upward of $27,000 per year per child. They made the situation work when only two children were of school age, but in the next academic year, there will be three children enrolled, and four not long after."

The letter continues, "The friends recently confided that they have applied for need-based scholarships for the three children, as they believe that their combined income is within the accepted range." Yet, the letter writer reports, the family regularly makes extravagant purchases of luxury goods, and otherwise demonstrates that they may have the money for tuition—if they stop spending it on impractical cars or paying retail for designer goods. The letter continues: "In the moment when they confided this, I didn't know how to respond. So I joked that perhaps the wife shouldn't take her $7,000 designer bag or wear the shoes and jewelry she had on to the interview. She laughed and said she would 'dress down' for the meeting." The letter concludes by asking whether the letter-writer should call out her friends on their deceptive behavior, and discourage it.

The Ethicist's answer goes on to excuse the family's behavior by saying the school will make the decision and that "eligibility requirements, properly designed, don't shut out poor families by allowances made to better-off applicants." The Ethicist also explains, "In cases where many or even most parents don't pay full fees, the sticker price can be thought of as a surcharge on the wealthy."[66] But, I couldn't help but think that the couple depicted in this letter perfectly illustrates the difference between those who take and those who make. If a family can afford a $7,000 handbag, surely they are the "wealthy" for whom this "surcharge" is intended—unless, of course, it's inconvenient for them to economize. A lot of liberal, redistributive policy depends on the idea that higher earners will step up to pay for benefits for those lower down on the income scale, but that system falls apart when those higher earners try to pass responsibility even further up, revealing the shocking lack of personal accountability that the system fosters.

Whether you have kids who need a better education, or your housekeeper doesn't want extra hours because she'll lose her food stamps, or you are simply tired of seeing other people skate through life snatching handouts while you work hard and hold yourself to higher standards, the need for personal accountability is clear. Women are often pressured into being "team players," but the team doesn't work if each person doesn't arrive with a strong sense of personal responsibility. As we've said, there's no "I" in "team," but there is a "me."

As a young woman whose personal politics were fairly unexamined, it took many years and many trials to fully realize the weight of that statement. When I graduated college, I never dreamed I'd go on welfare. I felt terrible about it but was only beginning to understand why. Then I went to the White House and learned about the kind of service and personal accountability that allowed people to thrive. But my experience culminated as a mother, when I learned how my choices intimately shape a life outside my own. I realized that my code of conduct, whether it was in the jobs I chose or the values I upheld or the decisions that led to starting my family, was built on a framework of personal accountability. This philosophy of personal accountability underpinned my daily actions, my approach to government, and even my respect for my own body. I had laid the cornerstone of my conservative approach to life.

Every woman knows the importance of making her own decisions, taking ownership of the consequences, and demonstrating respect for others. It's hard to get far in this world if we don't take responsibility to chart our own paths, and if we don't treat others well along the way. Personal accountability is the lining of our country's social fabric. We need to be empowered as citizens not only to make decisions for our own good, but also because the expectation that one makes decisions with respect for others upholds a civility that, until now, has not been as evident anywhere else in the world and is dangerously eroding.

In order to be civil to those around us, we first have to be aware of ourselves, along with our actions and their consequences. The woman who pushed past you at the sample sale didn't show a lot of self-awareness or responsibility for her actions. You were able to rise above it and continue your day with the same civil and thoughtful demeanor with which you approach all your interactions because you understand that your behavior plays a part in creating a responsible and respectful society. We need public policies that support that attitude, as well.

Our society needs to foster a sense of personal accountability and civility toward one another in order to thrive. It's not only possible for personal accountability to coexist with compassion and nurturing—they need each other.

Chapter 2

Financial Independence

As women, we are the Chief Everything Officers of our lives. More women own businesses than ever before (29% of business owners and rising),[1] matriculate from medical or law school (47% of medical school matriculants,[2] and 47% of law school matriculants),[3] and are the breadwinners of their households (a record 40% of households as of 2013).[4] Women are savvy and independent, and we know how to get what we want out of our lives and careers. Every day, we make important decisions: whether to invest in our kids' education or splurge on renovating our bathroom, how to maximize the return on investment in our company's new endeavor, or how to structure our retirement. The same principles we use to manage our own personal financial resources work on a larger scale in our economy through the exercise of fiscal policy.

Fiscal policy sounds so, well, "Washingtonian." We hear about it on the news and know it's a big deal, but how does it really impact us, day to day? It's pretty simple: countries and states need to balance their income (revenue) and spending (expenses) just like we do with our household or business budgets. Otherwise, they borrow too much and we all know the stress a pile of credit card (or any other) debt adds. It feels great when we have access to the credit to make that purchase, but not so great a few months later when we realize we can't pay for it in full and so the amount we owe just keeps getting bigger and bigger.

I've seen this play out on the personal *and* national levels, and I know intimately how a nation's debt affects the lives of all its citizens, whether they realize it or not. Two adventures in my life tell that parallel story: first, my experience in the White House managing the national debt of Iraq revealed how a policy that seems remote from average daily life actually touches every aspect of it; and then, when I started my own business (with the goal of empowering other young women), I learned a whole new definition of financial responsibility on an individual level. Before these experiences, I had been taught my whole life to make sound financial decisions, but these two periods of my life revealed the consequences of straying from financial conservatism in shocking detail, and taught me more than a lifetime's worth of lessons about hard decisions and economization.

The Power of America's Purse

Fiscal policy is simply the government's plan to manage its revenue (primarily taxes collected from us) and spending (the money the government puts toward health care and social security benefits, salaries for employees, etc.). Fiscal policy is the sorority sister to monetary policy, through which a central bank (in our case, The Federal Reserve Bank) manages and influences a nation's money supply. Together, these two types of policy aim to ensure a stable and, hopefully, prosperous economy.[5] (We'll dive into monetary policy in the next chapter.)

Historically, the government pretty much left economic policy alone in an approach to the economy called *laissez-faire*, or free markets. But after the Great Depression, politicians and economists determined that the government must be more involved in regulating business, employment, inflation, and money. These policy-shapers hoped to avert another nationwide financial catastrophe.

The philosophy behind modern fiscal policy, also known as Keynesian economics, stems from the theories of British economist John Maynard Keynes, a sort of Albert Einstein meets Donald Trump type (really, Google a photo of his hair). Keynes found that by tinkering with the amount of tax the government charges its citizens and businesses, along with its own spending level, government could influence the economy's productivity and, ultimately, growth. But achieving the right balance of taxation and spending is as fickle as your hot co-worker down the hall who's been in an on-and-off again relationship with his high school sweetheart for a decade. Too much taxation and spending chokes off business formation and growth, along with our ability to have an extra dollar in our pockets. Too little taxation and spending hinders the government from having critical resources to fund itself.

Fiscal policy gets complicated quickly, but, at its core, it's really about: (1) the amount of revenue government decides to collect, and from whom (i.e., who is taxed and at what rate); (2) how that revenue is allocated and spent by the government (i.e., defense spending or unemployment benefits); (3) what type of economic growth is expected from that spending (i.e., more job creation or better schools); and (4) what balance of the revenue and spending best stabilizes the economy (i.e., so items don't get too expensive).

When did government spending begin to surge? It's a complicated question, and the truth is, it's hard to say because inflation and other factors make it difficult to compare the federal budget of one year or decade to another from the past. But the trend has definitely been an upward one. A major spike in government outlays can be seen in 1941—understandable, as America entered World War II. However, spending never went back down to its previous levels, and instead began to steadily and precipitously increase, even after the war.[6] In the past twenty years alone, spending has grown 63 percent faster than inflation.[7] And, since the 1960s, we've seen a dramatic shift in how that money is spent, as well, going from about 50 percent spent on defense in 1962, to 22 percent in 2011, and seeing significant proportional increases in spending on Social Security, Medicare, Medicaid, and safety net programs.

One explanation for the rapid expansion of government spending could be the predominance of entitlements. Entitlements fall under what we call "mandatory spending," because the amount of money the government budgets for them is determined by the number of people who are eligible for the promised benefits or programs (not by the typical appropriations process in which Congress reviews individual programs and their merits and then portions out money for them). Currently, the amount our government pays into mandatory spending programs is more than twice that spent on discretionary programs.[8] This reveals another danger of "set it and forget it" entitlements programs—there's no place for their budgets to go but up, until they eventually become totally unsustainable.

Entitlements are programs that provide benefits to citizens, such as Social Security and healthcare market subsidies. These differ from welfare in that they aren't means-tested—they aren't there as a safety net in case of grave need, but instead they're offered to everyone, hence why we call them "entitlements"—we're all entitled to them as taxpayers. That makes it sound like the taxes we pay into entitlements come right back to us, right? The problem is, they don't. Like a pyramid scheme, many current entitlements are only sustainable if we keep feeding more and more taxpayer money into them. If you were around for the Bernie Madoff scandal, then you know how that ends. One day the pyramid is bound to collapse, and the U.S. is borrowing ever-increasing sums to try and postpone that day. Entitlements, unlike infrastructure improvements, national security, or schools, are a government investment in which the societal benefits cannot ever exceed the costs, because that money becomes immediately liquidated. When this money is syphoned out of the economy with little or no hope of encouraging growth, debt may seem like the only way to keep our financial ship afloat. But unlike building schools or roads, liquidating money into entitlements doesn't yield clear results for the overall social good.

When the government spends more, it needs to cover its costs (i.e., its credit card bill). To cover its costs, the Treasury can either raise taxes on some people, or all people. The government can also increase taxes on some or all businesses. If the government raises taxes on businesses, businesses need to find a way to cover the costs of those taxes, such as any combination of: moving away to a less-taxed locale (perhaps even another country, or "offshore"), reducing jobs and/or salaries, or investing less in product growth. Fewer jobs and lower wages mean individuals feel the financial pinch; when the government raises business, or corporate, taxes, it's not "just businesses' problem," it quickly becomes everybody's problem.

Think about the goods and services we depend on every day, as we go about our jobs as Chief Everything Officers. Many of these goods and services perform double-duty, whether we realize it or not. For example, owning an energy-efficient TV isn't just a neat way to watch Netflix with the whole family; it's also saving on energy bills, which improves our ability to spend or save that money elsewhere. The high-powered vacuum that keeps our homes neat and hygienic is the result of companies spending decades in product research and development, and not only does it do a good job cleaning our places, it also saves us hundreds of hours of time and effort compared to the way women used to keep their homes clean before vacuums. The time we get back from those tasks is worth money, too. But taxing businesses at high levels cuts into the money *they* have available for product development (or simply drives up the costs of those products to the consumer), costing us not just the opportunity to own a neat gadget, but also all the time and effort that neat gadget might have saved us. Some economists even go so far as to theorize that the development of increasingly efficient home appliances played an integral role in women's liberation.[9] Businesses' ability to continue developing such products and offering them at affordable prices is directly impacted by their tax burden.

In addition to, or instead of, raising taxes, the government can also borrow money. Have you ever seen one of those huge billboards with the enormous multi-trillion dollar number ticking upwards every second to reflect the huge size and rapid increase of our national debt? Even if one doesn't know exactly what the number represents, it can make one's heart pound to look at its rapid increase. So, just how are spending, taxes, and that national debt related? When the government spends more than it collects in taxes from citizens and businesses, it needs to borrow.

Think of the national debt we hear so much about no differently than we think about our own credit card, mortgage, auto loan or student debt. Today, the United States owes $18.8 trillion dollars. Of that amount, $5.2 trillion is what we call intergovernmental holdings, or money allocated for government obligations to citizens (such as Social Security payments), and $13.6 trillion is public debt, or money owed to bondholders, often from other countries like China.[10] Just like many individuals do, when the US Treasury needs money to cover its spending obligations, it borrows. In the case of the Treasury, it borrows money from investors (like banks, investment firms and other countries' governments). In exchange for the money, the US Treasury makes a promise to repay the sum originally borrowed ("the principal"), plus some additional funds for the privilege of borrowing (the "interest"). Treasury acceptance of this loan and its promise to repay the money plus the additional fees at a later date is called a bond.

When someone buys a government bond, they're basically giving the government a loan, which they will collect on later, with interest. This was long considered one of the least risky methods of investing and growing money in America, which is why you may remember receiving bonds as gifts on graduation, or perhaps even at birth—the idea being that by the time you were old enough to collect on the bond, it will have accrued lots of juicy interest! Of course, the dependability of bonds is based on the assumption that America's economy, and the American government's "good credit score," is rock-solid. Is that really true all the time? One way to find out is to look at the interest rate that our government's creditors charge us. And that interest rate affects more than just the people who directly borrow from, or lend to, the government.

When the government borrows more, investors can get worried about when or how they'll get paid back, so they charge the government high rates to borrow from them. As interest rates rise, it means that money costs more for many others who need it, like businesses, who borrow money all the time, and prospective homebuyers, who want to borrow for a mortgage. In other words, America's borrowing problem becomes everyone's borrowing problem.

When I had the privilege of serving at the White House, one of the key imperatives for ensuring American safety and prosperity was assisting Iraq in stabilizing their economy. What was bringing that nation down financially was one of the world's largest national debts. A problem that seems remote to us was affecting the daily lives of that nation's citizens, from their access to health care to their ability to hold down a stable job. Iraq isn't the only place where this could happen, however. Numbers don't lie. A debt is a debt, and massive debt can—and will—threaten any nation if left unchecked.

What the media failed miserably to portray back in 2003 and 2004 is that the US and its allies were helping Iraq make tremendous progress after the ouster of Saddam Hussein. With a constitution in place and a (albeit tenuous) security plan, businesses were beginning to re-open, banks were forming, and hospitals were resuming care. But, for years, Saddam Hussein had taken incredibly huge amounts of money from other countries and never paid it back. By 2003, Iraq owed a lot of countries money; in fact, with an estimated $120 billion in debt, Iraq was one of the most heavily indebted nations ever. No country wanted to invest in the new Iraq until its old debts were taken care of; in other words, countries that were willing to invest wanted to be sure they had a chance to get their money back, let alone see it earn an investment return.

In 2003, World Bank President James Wolfensohn said that Iraq's debts needed to be reduced by 33% in order to pay for reconstruction needs and sustained economic development.[11]

President George W. Bush recognized the importance of this dilemma and, in December 2003, appointed one of our country's most respected and accomplished diplomats as his Special Presidential Envoy (SPE) for Iraq Debt Relief. A Special Presidential Envoy is, essentially, a personal representative of the President, a position typically reserved for those highly critical scenarios that require Presidential-level representation while engaging with worldwide leaders. It would have be hard to find someone more qualified for this role than James Addison Baker III, who served as the Chief of Staff for two Presidents, and as both Secretary of the Treasury and Secretary of State.

Over the course of the next year, I was honored to be part of a small team serving the President, National Security Advisor Condoleezza Rice, and Secretary Baker on Iraq debt relief. With Secretary Baker, we developed a strategy and traveled the world to meet with the likes of Presidents and Crown Princes in hopes of gaining an international consensus to forgive Iraq's Debt and enable the country to start anew, economically. On November 21, 2004, just eleven months after Secretary Baker became SPE, the Paris Club, an organization of countries that work to solve the payment problems of indebted nations, agreed on a debt relief program for Iraq, agreeing to forgive 80% of Iraq's debt. Anyone who has any familiarity with Washington policy-making will appreciate how virtually unheard of it is to conceive of and enact a policy requiring broad international consensus in less than a year. President Bush, National Security Advisor Rice and Secretary Baker demonstrated not only the power of important ideas and planning, but also the power of diplomacy.

By 2007, inflation in Iraq had begun to decrease and the IMF projected economic growth of 7–10 percent.[12] Plenty of improvements remained to be seen, but reducing the national debt of Iraq was instrumental in promoting the positive strides that were made in what was really a very short time since the removal of Saddam Hussein just a few years prior.

Iraq is an extreme example, but it goes to show what unchecked debt can do to a nation, in ways that trickle down to the average citizen's spending power, employment prospects, access to basic services such as health care, and ultimately, even stability and security. And, it goes to show how powerful low debt can be by fostering an environment ripe for prosperity.

Playing Musical Chairs with Income

Liberals want to take care of everyone with benefits or handouts, and handouts aren't free. The government needs to have enough income to pay for them, and the government doesn't earn money like you or I—it has to get it from someone else. That "someone else" is going to be the average taxpayer, now *and* when America's credit card bill (the national debt) comes due. Instead of handing out borrowed "success," conservatives say we should hand out opportunity for people to create their own success.

Handouts don't work on a social and practical level; they wear down the sense of individual responsibility, and many of these programs aren't held to high standards of accountability and success. Importantly, these programs also don't work on an economic level. The money the government spends comes from three sources: taxing citizens and businesses, borrowing from investors (sometimes called "deficit financing"), and printing new money; however, each of these have important costs and consequences to consider.

Take a look at borrowing, for starters. There's always a lot of chatter about China and our national debt. Foreign holders of American government debt didn't start to become very common until the 1970s, but they've grown steadily since. Today, China holds almost 14% of our debt. Japan holds just slightly less than China, but after them, the next largest single nation's holding is 4%.[13]

Does this matter? It does, because we all know the implication of the phrase "the power of the purse strings." When we owe others money, that gives them power over us. For instance, they could demand favors, or stop lending us money, or attach conditions to their loan that affect how we can use the money. Does any of this matter to us, the individual taxpayers? Think about it this way: you go on a date. You are *not* into it. The check comes. You request to split it, because that makes you feel more comfortable than feeling indebted to a near-stranger—especially one you aren't planning on seeing again. But your date refuses to let you contribute, snatching the bill out of your hand. He wants to make you feel like you are more on the hook to go on the second date. When people pay for us or lend us money, we feel beholden to them (or, at least, they hope we do). Have you ever been friends with someone who was planning a wedding, who took money from family to help pay for it, but then had to incorporate that family member's opinions into all their wedding decisions? If you thought handling a demanding mother-in-law was delicate, imagine someone with that power not only over you but also over an entire economy, expecting to have his or her way.

So, what if we wanted to pay off our country's debt and ensure our independence and growth trajectory? Simple. We each—and

I mean *every*—one of us, including every baby just born this minute, need to come up with $57,782. Or, if we want to ensure we pay all of our debts, including future obligations (the way a publicly traded company is required to report to its shareholders), we each need to come up with the humble sum of $232,627.[14] Not going to happen? I didn't think so. So, instead, we should come up with some pretty savvy policy solutions because, I don't know about you, but I'd like to keep what's in my new eBay-purchased Coach handbag. As long as the national debt exists as it does now, a whopping seven percent of our entire federal budget is spent *just paying interest on the money our government borrows*.[15] As women's incomes rise[16] and more and more women are becoming the bread-winners for their families,[17] women have more cause than ever to care deeply about where our hard-earned tax dollars are going. And a recent survey demonstrated that Millennials fear tax season more than any other group, showing particular concerns about the complexity of their taxes and their ability to get a substantial refund.[18] That's not surprising, given that in addition to being the newest cohort of tax-payers in America, they also face rising taxes in a tough job market, while more and more layers of complexity keep being piled onto the tax code to supposedly correct the ills that these high taxes have caused.

What's an alternative to taking on more debt if we keep up this spending? Higher taxes for everyone, and increasingly higher taxes the more money a person makes, in a process called "income redistribution." Remember that supposed Churchill quote about liberals with hearts becoming conservatives with brains? Income redistribution works really well in theory (and sounds great, too—who doesn't want to be Robin Hood?) until we make a little bit of money. But, then we'd like to keep our money, right? Let's say we each earn a million dollars tomorrow. We then need to pay the following taxes: $88,200 (8.82%) to New York State for the privilege of living and working there, $39,200 to New York City for the same privilege, and $345,550 (39.6%) to the federal government. The income tax we will pay will be $472,950, or 47.3% of what we've just earned! And, the grand total will be even more because we'll also need to pay the payroll, Social Security, and Medicare taxes associated with our earned income.

Our wallets are probably smarting—and so is our spirit. After all, that is not only 47% of our money, but also 47% of the effort, time, passion, and hard work we put into earning it, down the black hole of government spending. A Pew Study found that, between two generations, the daughters saw an increase of three times more earnings than their mothers had in the labor force.[19] Imagine how much more that will be when the daughters of the millennial generation enter the economy. At our current trajectory, how much of *their* hard-earned money will wind up paying off American debt or bankrolling wasteful government programs? That kind of high taxation is unsustainable. And even liberals agree this is a problem.

During the financial decline of 2008, the liberal Center for American Progress wrote that "for many years in this country it was understood that as worker productivity rose, the benefits of that increase should be shared equally between workers and their employers. [It is] one of the cardinal rules of economic growth—if we want output and profits to grow, we have to have consumers with the buying power to purchase those products."[20] Their study promoted labor laws and redistributive taxes in order to share the wealth between workers and employers, but the very same argument could be made *against* draconian taxes, because they inhibit the purchasing power of far more people than only the nation's most wealthy—just look at the disappearing middle class.

High taxes do more harm than just the obvious direct consequences of reducing *everyone's* spending power. Progressive taxation also throws a serious wrench in the works when it comes to how we view, reward, and encourage success.

Progressive taxation is a method of taxation that is supposed to fine-tune the redistributive process by taxing the wealthy at a higher rate than the poor. You might have heard people talk about it by referring to "taxing the one percent." In theory, that sounds nice; solve that pesky issue of taxes hurting people's spending power by only taxing the rich super high rates (because they can afford it and keep spending!) while taxing the poor and the middle class at a lower rate (so they can take their money to the bank, the mall, the tuition fund, the mortgage office). Problem solved, right? I think we all know what comes after "in theory" by now.

One reason this system isn't working is it requires the federal government to define "rich," "poor," and "middle class" in sweeping terms that really don't mean much to anybody anymore. How? Well, part of the problem is that the feds define "rich" and "poor" by broad goalposts—earn more than x per year, and you qualify for this income bracket, which raises or lowers your tax rate accordingly. But, a family's quality of life is determined by more than just a single number on its paystubs; it's determined by the spending power of that money. Two families, in completely different parts of the country, can earn the same exact income; yet, one family might be struggling to make ends meet, while the other lives comfortably. That's because, among states, the cost of common goods and services can vary by up to 32 percentage points, and rents can vary in price by up to 97 percentage points.[21] In other words, the same apartment that rents for $1000 per month in Phoenix, Arizona might cost close to $2000 per month in New York City. And, that's just the differences between states—within states there can be vast differences between relatively rural areas and major metropolitan areas.

That family who, according to the federal definition, can totally afford a higher tax rate, might feel that higher tax rate a lot harder than we realize—and it's going to further damage their ability to contribute to the economy as spenders, too. Instead of taxing the rich and giving to the poor, we wind up taxing the already-struggling in a system that supposedly was created to encourage them to contribute more of their money to the economy!

There's another issue with this policy of progressive taxation, which is that in practice, the burden isn't as evenly shared as it sounds. According to recent studies, "The top 10 percent of income earners paid 68 percent of all federal income taxes in 2011 (the latest year available), though they earned 45 percent of all income. The bottom 50 percent paid 3 percent of income taxes, but earned 12 percent of income."[22] In other words, the tax burden disparity exceeds the disparity in income. According to estimates of the current tax disparity, made by the nonpartisan Tax Policy Center, "the top 20 percent of earners in the US are paying more than 80 percent of income taxes."[23] And an increasingly large group of those top earners are women: while women are still struggling against the "glass ceiling" in the business world, the proportion of female top earners has been rising steadily and rapidly in the last thirty years, going from about two percent in the eighties to more than ten percent today.[24] But whether the money's coming from male or female earners, that's a relatively small group of people paying for a big chunk of government—which uncovers yet another problem with big government spending: it's hard to crystalize voter support behind cutting spending, however necessary it might be, if more people benefit from programs than those who feel the heat on their tax bills. Who doesn't want a free lunch?

Here's something we can all agree on: it hurts to see a world in which some people barely scrape together the nutrition and warm clothes they need to survive while others seem to revel in financial excess. It's natural that we long to improve the fate of those who are suffering, and it seems like an easy solution to do so by pinching off just a bit of that excess and sharing it down. It's not that simple, unfortunately. Taxing the "rich" may actually be hurting the poor by reducing the ability of wealthier citizens to invest in the capital necessary to create jobs; according to one expert, "It takes about $200,000 of nonresidential assets to support one average job."[25] Suddenly that millionaire doesn't seem so rich; even if they didn't need their wealth to support themselves, it would only pay for the capital required to create five jobs. Those five jobs, however, can support five more people, if the millionaire is permitted to keep and invest his or her money. The government return on investment isn't very attractive: about $0.40 of every dollar collected in taxes is absorbed into the costs of collection and disbursement into programs, meaning one dollar of your tax money will be transformed into $0.60 of government services, at best.[26] When the government is using that money to build roads or schools, the societal benefit of those services can be felt immediately, and for a long time. However, when that money goes into entitlements (as a substantial and increasing portion of it does!), the benefits will never, ever exceed the costs. Even outside entitlements, government investment rarely exceeds the value added of private investment; while government spending is necessary and good in some instances (such as building infrastructure), it's not the most efficient way to grow the economy.

Progressive income tax also comes with a moral hazard: discouraging and punishing hard work and success. If everyone pays income tax—even if it's just five cents—that at least means everyone has skin in the game. When we vote, we all feel the effects of the policies our elected officials support, both the costs and the benefits. Shifting more and more of the tax burden onto a smaller and smaller group of people isn't just bad economics; it's bad for society. So, some liberals say, let's tax *businesses*. Corporations aren't people, right? Or so we hear. The problem is, high corporate taxes (when they're enforceable at all) have the same effect as high income taxes—they discourage growth and innovation, and reroute money into programs that offer a less efficient cost-to-benefit ratio. Plus, corporations are *owned* by people, so taxing what seems like an impersonal entity is still, by extension, taxing real people who are going to feel the hit. In reality, however, the real reason these taxes don't work is that they're virtually unenforceable. Corporations have many ways to avoid taxation by changing their official place of business—meaning high corporate taxes wind up *costing* America by encouraging businesses to relocate offshore.

Unfortunately, if high taxes weren't enough, an unstable fiscal environment (like the kind created by large national debt) discourages investment, meaning replacing those taxes with more debt isn't the answer, either. As Walter Williams writes, "Except in many instances when government rigs the game with crony capitalism, income is mostly a result of one's productivity and the value people place on that productivity."[27] In other words, while income redistribution sounds like an easy fix, the fact of the matter is if we want to raise people's incomes, we have to help them earn more themselves—and that's going to involve leaving wealth in the hands of those who can use it to create jobs, and creating a stable financial environment in which they can grow, invest, and share that wealth through productivity.

Some liberal economists have argued that higher marginal tax rates correlate to periods of growth in GDP,[28] yet even they are reluctant to fully claim causation, and their arguments for the social benefit of high taxes on the rich are further rebuffed by evidence that during the same periods of increased redistribution, income inequality in America actually increased.[29] A look at the numbers reveals that, in the 1980s and 90s, the economy expanded at unprecedented levels—right when government expenditure shrank to one-fifth of the gross domestic product.[30] That shouldn't be a surprise given that income redistribution simply moves existing income around, but is a highly inefficient way to grow more money.

This issue is more urgent than ever because of recent hikes in government spending, the infamous "Stimulus Bill" of 2009. That year wasn't actually the start of government spending increases—they hit a sharp incline in 2007, reaching nearly 30 percent of our gross domestic product—nearly one third of all the money generated in the United States![31] History has shown that spending on this level doesn't generate growth—look at the hikes of the 1930s, 60s, and 70s, which failed to increase the rate of growth. Troublingly, history and thorough research shows that women suffer uniquely in economic downturns, often resulting in setbacks in women's equality in the workforce and, in some cases, even their access to schooling or health care.[32] Yet we seem to be walking the same road again, unless we change things now.

Of course, not all government spending is bad and some is even critical, like defense spending to ensure our safety. America proudly has a strong record of investing in innovation, not only via the private sector, but also through the government. Initial investments by the government of millions of dollars in the 1950s and 60s have yielded billions of dollars and important innovations, like the Global Position System (GPS), safer drinking water, and better cancer therapies.[33]

Despite government's real spending needs, the reallocation of capital is disastrous, economically and psychologically. In practice, this is where personal accountability meets financial independence. We can never be economically stable if we're taking from others, and liquidating wealth where we should be growing it— not as individuals, or as a nation. If my time in the White House weren't enough, I had another opportunity to make some of the hardest financial decisions of my life, decisions that really drove this lesson home, when I started my company, Startiste.

Moving On Up in America

Growing up in an entrepreneurial family, I was raised on the idea that doing for one's self was the epitome of success. My dad was an entrepreneur, his mother and father were entrepreneurs, his mother's father was an entrepreneur, and so on. I had known all along that one day I would be an entrepreneur as well and, with corporate and policy experience under my belt, 2005 seemed a good as time as any to embark on this journey.

Before starting my own business, I had worked as a venture capitalist, so I had seen first-hand the struggles of trying to raise money for a startup. If I had a dollar for every management team in khakis and a blue button-down shirt who told me their start-up would have revenues of $50 thousand, $300 thousand, $2.5 million and more than $10 million, respectively, for each of the next four years, I'd be a very rich gal! Unfortunately, it is all too rare for a start-up to meet that type of revenue projection. But, I understood that kind of vision and ambition is what was required to get a business off the ground—entrepreneurs need big hopes and dreams, because if they don't believe it's possible first, no one else will help them *make it* possible. And coming from my own family background of big dreams and hard work, it was thrilling to see so many brave and passionate people jump into the fray of business ownership. However, as an investor, I had seen firsthand too many start-up management teams take money into their companies when a return on that capital was highly unlikely. It's not a perfect science, but I had a responsibility to make sure that the businesses we invested in would be able to not only earn our money back, but also earn a return. It's hard being the voice of reality and I had to make some tough calls, turning down businesses even when some of them seemed to have huge potential—and actually went on to hit it big!

As a venture investor, it is tempting to fund every good idea but, ultimately, it is critical to understand your risk parameters for any investment, and stay true to those parameters; doing so makes dealing with the losses much more reasonable. I learned two critically important lessons from my boss about managing risk when I was a mortgage bond trader: First, never let your heart get in the way of a trade (or an economic risk you are taking) for you won't be able to make rational economic decisions; and second, always set your absolute rock bottom loss level upfront, and cut off the trade when that level is reached. (So if you buy a share of stock for $100 but are not willing to lose more than $20, you sell that share when it hits $80. You don't sit there and wait to see if its price rises again because it could, instead, continue to drop.)

So when I was finally ready to launch my own business, I knew what kind of investment environment I was entering, and I had already internalized some tough lessons about taking other people's money. Now, it was time to make *my* dream come true!

I had long held a dream of creating a business that empowered young girls. I'd forged my ideas during the years that I developed a leadership training program for a high school in New York City, and while I volunteered as a mentor in my corporate roles. Educating young women, mentoring them in leadership, and giving them the tools they needed to be successful and make history was a passion of mine. Finally, I started Startiste, a create-your-own retail experience for girls. At Startiste, girls could design their own crafts and products using our online tool, then pick up the final product in the store. Each project they could complete was tied to an empowering theme, telling stories of important woman from history, and encouraging girls to blossom as leaders and innovators.

I felt strongly that I didn't want to start a business on borrowed money, so I chose to seek venture capital instead. In venture capital, investors give entrepreneurs the startup funds they need, in exchange for a share of the company. The idea is that as the company rises in value, so will the value of the shares, eventually earning back the money that was invested and even turning a good profit for the investor. Rather than loaning entrepreneurs money, venture capitalists actually *buy* a portion of their startup companies up front, so these investors became co-owners of Startiste. This was the kind of transaction I'd overseen for several years. I was ready, and I was armed with a meticulously detailed plan.

In just six months, from raising capital to launch day, we did the unthinkable: we designed a one-of-a-kind retail store and web experience, created product components that enabled more than 4 million real-time designs, and trained a team of high school and college girls to become one of the most effective sales teams in the mall. Our site was up and running, we were getting national media attention, we had a prime spot in one of the toniest malls in America, and then disaster struck.

Just a couple of weeks after we opened, the financial crisis occurred. Mall traffic fell off a cliff. You could hear a pin drop in the mall. We tried to persevere, and our metrics told a good story. But, in essence, I knew too much. Business was doing well, but the costs of regulation and compliance, coupled with a bad economy, were challenging. From my days managing venture capital, I knew there were much more compelling investment options out there in the marketplace beyond tween retail, and especially mall-based retail. Retail guru Andrew Rosen, the esteemed founder of Theory, warned me about mall-based retail when I showed him my plan. Clearly, I should have listened better. After a heartbreaking soul search, I recommended to our investors that we look for another CEO, who I would be happy to train and transition, or we should close.

If losing one's own money is tough, try losing other people's money. I didn't sleep for months; my hair fell out in clumps and my skin looked like an enemy army had invaded and built bunkers on it. Our investors understood, and believed we had encountered extraordinary circumstances due to the financial crisis, but I couldn't shake the feeling I had failed. Fortunately, I had included a fairly atypical, albeit expensive cancellation clause in our lease for the mall space, one of those "just in case" risk-management measures I had learned from my own venture capital days. I exercised it, and gave the mall the appropriate notice. Then, against everyone's recommendation, I told the young men and women who worked for us that we would be closing in the coming months. They were high school and college students, for most of whom this was their first job. *Everyone* told me not to tell my employees; that if I did they would quit and I would have no one to run the store in the last months. But I knew that if I was fair, they would stand by me. I had trained these kids, been tough on them, and walked the walk with them through 2:00 a.m. openings on Black Friday, through endless all-nighters unpacking pallets of inventory in the dungeons of the mall, and more. Blinking back tears, I explained to them what had transpired: how we were being impacted by the economic downturn, and why I thought it was the most prudent decision to close our business. And, I made them a promise that I would not take a job myself until every single one of them got a new job. In the end, not one single employee left until that store was empty and the doors were shut. Not one. In fact, from that day onwards until the end, we were actually over-staffed, as employees who were not on the schedule that day "stopped by" to lend a helping hand.

It turned out that Startiste was the story of the American Dream, just a different one: a dream of American character, values, and civility. Not every business succeeds, and not every investment blossoms into riches. I had to accept these truths in a deeply personal way. But I also learned that hard work, loyalty, supportiveness, and enrichment could coexist with these difficult experiences. I had still succeeded in my goal of empowering girls—I had provided them an example of real-life business decisions, and I had shown them how to handle life's hardest moments and recover to try again one day—skills every woman must have.

And, I learned that the great entrepreneurs don't just have to have ideas and execution know-how; they also need the ability to power through doubt to keep grinding away. In retrospect, I think I'm a bit too practical to be a great entrepreneur of a start-up company, and I vowed that never again would I start a business with anything but my own money. But, I did find my strengths in leadership and in growing ideas, and in giving girls, including myself, a voice.

This experience, along with my time working on the Iraq debt crisis in the White House, took my existing respect for financial responsibility and made me realize that it was about much more than the money. Financial responsibility is about respect and empowerment—respect for the ways in which our own financial decisions ripple outward to affect those around us, and empowerment through the good that we can perpetuate through our wise financial choices. When viewed that way, financial responsibility is way bigger than just a few numbers shifting between columns, and way more personal than it seems when we flip on CSPAN for yet another droning speech on balancing the national budget.

Closing my business wasn't an easy decision, financially or emotionally. I was afraid not only of seeming like a failure, myself, but also of letting down my employees. However, I worked hard to make sure they were on the path to building up their careers beyond the company, while saving my investors years of potential losses or stagnation. It took this cutback in order to set everyone on the path of growth again. Ultimately, I realized that not only was this the wise decision to make, but it was also the compassionate one.

Reforming government spending is similar; on first blush, it sounds like it would hurt more people than it would help. On the one hand, we'd get those cold numbers on their charts into a better state; but on the other hand, it means people would have to go without some of the programs and services they depended on, and that doesn't sound very nice. However, in the long run, out-of-control government spending, and the national debt and high taxation that fund it, wind up hurting far more people to a much higher degree than cutting back does. In fact, cutting back on government spending doesn't just help our government's financial state; it can wind up helping those same people who might see a decline in their benefits and entitlements, if it means the money that remains in the government's pocket is being funneled into programs with high accountability and an emphasis on getting people back on their own two feet, and the money that *isn't* taxed anymore is re-deployed to revitalize the economy.

That's why I support free markets: because they offer more opportunity for everyone. But free markets can only exist if we eliminate the reallocation of wealth that's so dangerous to our society—and corrosive to the checks on government power. Innovation and growth depend on people's ability to invest their money into capital and business development, while other people are free to spend their money on the products and services thus created. Reallocation doesn't work, financially or morally. It creates a system in which a small group of taxpayers are bearing the bulk of the tax burden for programs benefiting a much wider group who never feel the financial burn of the services they consume. Without personal financial accountability, those people have no good reason to vote for the spending diet our country so sorely needs. When we vote for programs and the politicians who support them, we're really voting for where the money in our wallets will go. That's why it's critical, for our republic to function well, for all citizens to contribute *something*—not simply to rely on the Robin Hood method of taxing the richest at exorbitantly high rates while millions of other Americans scarcely feel the financial consequences of their voting decisions.

There are several conservative remedies that offer an alternative to progressive, redistributive taxation, while still funding our government at an acceptable level. One controversial idea is the "flat tax"—removing the "bracket" system we have in place now for income taxation, and instead taxing everyone at the same flat, low rate. Proponents argue that a flat tax would remove disincentives to success, because your tax rate won't rise as your income does.[34] Plus, it means that *everyone* has skin in the game, hopefully leading to wiser voting (and, by extension, federal spending) decisions. Not every conservative solution to income redistribution is this radical, however; many other conservatives simply argue for lower rates within the existing bracket system. Another proposed conservative remedy is formally referred to as the "Fair Tax" (as opposed to the flat tax or the progressive tax). The "Fair Tax" does away with income taxation and replaces it with a tax on consumption, similar to the United Kingdom's VAT but with a few major differences that have never been attempted anywhere else in the world.[35] The "Fair Tax" proposal is hotly debated for many reasons, one of which is its novelty, but also because consumption taxes are sometimes seen as prohibitive to growth as income taxes can be, and other people are concerned that they could prevent needy families from purchasing the goods they require.

At the end of the day, while each conservative remedy to our current progressive tax system is subject to lots of debate and contestation, they all demonstrate one very important point: there is another way for the American government to raise the money it needs to provide the services required of it. And we need creative solutions now more than ever, as spending burgeons to historic highs.

Income redistribution is really just a way of trying to postpone the inevitable realization that the federal government is spending far more than America can afford. Whatever we wind up doing to fix the tax code, we also need to curb government spending. In less than 15 years, federal spending per household has grown almost 30 percent.[36] It's time for America to put the credit card in the freezer like Rebecca in *Confessions of a Shopaholic*. We can start by fixing entitlements so our children actually stand a shot of having more than we do. Social Security and healthcare market subsidies account for nearly half of the federal budget; Social Security alone is 24% of federal spending.[37] As painful as entitlement reform might be, America simply doesn't have a stable, independent financial future without them. Without entitlement reform, we will never deliver on the promises of these programs; we will never truly care in a dignified manner for our elderly and our poor, and we will never be free of the enormous debt owed investor nations, like China.

Entitlements aren't just a financial hazard; they're a moral hazard as well. The same issues of discouraging personal responsibility and fostering dependence on government that we discussed last chapter when it came to welfare are also inherent dangers of widespread entitlements. There are other options, however. For example, some counties in Texas used a brief loophole to create a privatized version of Social Security that gave individuals more control over their retirement savings, while guaranteeing various tiers of payouts when contributors chose to retire (something Social Security doesn't do).[38] Other free-market financial innovations can help move the vital functions that many entitlements serve in people's lives into more localized, personalized programs that allow people to hold onto their own money and make the best use of it, while still protecting the nation's most vulnerable.

This kind of change isn't unprecedented on a national scale. Chile was the first nation in the Western Hemisphere to institute a Social Security-type national retirement system (in 1924), and by the 1970s they were facing all-too-familiar funding problems, so in 1981 they began the process of privatization.[39] The Chilean Social Security-type system was ultimately replaced by one in which workers invest in individual retirement accounts managed by private firms that compete for workers' business. This system has ensured that everyone has skin in the game while still promoting a secure retirement for all workers. As a result, the savings rate in Chile has more than doubled. Chile provides a good model for how to transition to a more privatized system of retirement assurance without leaving anyone out in the cold. As America's Baby

Boomer population ages, and our worker-to-retiree ratio gets closer and closer (meaning fewer workers are funding pensioners' retirement), such a transition cannot be delayed.

The final key component of reducing spending is bureaucratic reform at the government and state levels. This is never easy, given the vested interests that support every one of the government programs and agencies in our country. But here's an area in which the public sector can borrow some private sector ideas. Our political leaders must be willing to own the backlash of special interests, which may simply be a group of committed citizens, and look at our government structures more like corporations evaluate their various businesses in terms of measuring success, reforming and reengineering failed endeavors, and improving accountability actions to reduce waste and fraud.

Another way to protect people from misfortune is to just let them keep more of their money! Lower taxes for individuals and corporations means greater prosperity: let taxpayers keep more money in their pockets to spend on goods, build up equity in their homes, and start new businesses. While I believe (unlike redistributionist economists) that freedom is not free; *everyone* should pay taxes so we all share, and feel, the financial burden of our governance, that doesn't mean I want anybody to pay *too much* in taxes! Not only should the burden be more evenly spread, but with reduced spending, the entire burden should be reduced, as well. Currently, the IRS specifies seven tax brackets, depending on income and filing status: 10 percent, 15 percent, 25 percent, 28 percent, 33 percent, 35 percent, and 39.6 percent.[40] One of the most popular flat tax recommendations sets the flat rate at 20 percent for everyone, which is lower than the current median rate.

Lower taxes on individuals is just the start, though; corporate taxes need reform as well. America no longer consistently ranks as the best place to operate or start a business. We need to support pro-business policies that break down barriers to business. We need local and national reforms that allow both small and large businesses to thrive without heavy compliance costs for outdated or unnecessary laws. One way to do that will be through entitlement reform, which will also remove burdensome compliance costs from business owners. Stabilizing the national debt would also create a financial environment more conducive to investment and business creation. Reducing the national debt must be an extremely high priority in our next federal budget; there is no time to waste. As the popular saying goes, "The most powerful force in the universe is compound interest." It waits for no one.

Corporate tax rates (which were originally thought of as a solution to America's financial worries) have had the opposite effect, driving businesses out of the US and into "tax havens." The truth is, no matter what the corporate tax rate is, businesses will always seek to reduce their tax burden by any means possible; from the point of view of the owners and managers, it just makes financial sense. Raising corporate tax rates does little to fund American spending, but lowering them may actually improve America's fortunes by making America a more attractive place to headquarter a business.

A better business environment is good for everyone—owners, employees, and women everywhere. Our careers, our prosperity, and even our safety and national security depend on the financial good sense of our government.

Value Two: Financial Independence

There's a reason layaway is passé. Not to sound all Suze Orman, but it is a tough reality: we shouldn't buy what we can't afford. It always comes back to bite us. The hit show *Say Yes to the Dress* follows a bevvy of prospective brides as they shop for the perfect gown. One of the most common obstacles they face is budget: many brides have to decide whether they should break the bank for one moment of glamor. Instead of pushing women—and America—to say yes to the dress, we should say yes to success—through financial independence! We need free markets in which smart gals can start businesses, work from home, and follow their dreams without having to hand it all over to Uncle Sam once they earn it. We know that part of being a smart, sexy, successful woman is thinking past today and preparing for tomorrow. We don't splurge on Egyptian cotton sheets when we're struggling to keep a roof over our beds. But we work hard in the confidence that hard work pays off, because we live in a system where effort is rewarded, and financial stability is cultivated through wise choices by individuals. We've spent the economic downturn hunting for brands in T.J. Maxx, and now we can enjoy the benefits of our prudence while others scramble to look up the return policy on the Marchesa gown they bought on credit.

Financial independence is not an easy road to walk. I have experienced, in powerful and personal ways, the reality of the tough decisions that have to be made to maintain it. From managing the Iraq debt crisis to making the difficult call to shut my own business down, I've seen that financial independence isn't always fun or glamorous—but it is absolutely necessary for security and prosperity.

Individuals who are financially independent are happier and more successful. They have more freedom to do what they want, and they have more choices. America needs to rebuild a business environment in which everyone can thrive. And on that same principle, a nation that is financially independent is more free, which is why America needs to put her credit cards in the freezer.

In a nation that also fosters a sense of personal responsibility, financial independence is a natural complement to our first value. Financial independence isn't just a rat race. Wall Street and Main Street need to work together in order for everyone to succeed, as we'll see next. Teach a woman to fish and eventually you'll have the Barefoot Contessa!

Chapter 3

Investment in Opportunity

As Ms. Chief Everything Officer, we women also have to make long-term financial decisions. It's a no-brainer that we head to yoga because we know the long-term benefits are worth it, even if we would rather lounge on the couch and binge Netflix instead. We stay up late to make muffins for the new family down the street, because community is important. We understand how the "macro" of the world around us and our future is connected with the "micro" of our day-to-day actions and decisions, and we have a keen intuition for how investments today pay off in the long run. Our daily decisions—whether it's choosing to patronize the local coffee shop on the corner or forge a new business alliance— demonstrate that we understand how everyone's businesses, large and small, are intertwined.

When I launched my startup in 2006, I did everything from visiting vendors in a remote Chinese village to unpacking pallets in the basement of a mall in one of America's highest-income communities. I've seen firsthand how every level of our economy is connected. I've also observed my friends' lives and realized that the way we women go about our day-to-day business is a lot like the economy on a personal scale—governed by the same principles of interconnectivity, responsibility, and long-term vision.

My favorite scene from the book *The Devil Wears Prada* is the one in which Andy, the editor's uncomely assistant, gets caught smirking at the editor and her fashion director as they deliberate the optimal shade of a blue blouse being featured in the upcoming issue. Andy clearly thinks their obsession over color is inane and inconsequential. The editor haughtily reprimands Andy for thinking she is "above" such a menial task as deliberating the color of a shirt. The editor explains that Andy's selection of the blue sweater she wore that day was indeed a choice made not by Andy, but by the editor four years ago when she decided to feature cerulean blue fashion on the magazine's cover. That cerulean blue was then copied by Bloomingdales, who was copied by Old Navy, and so on all the way down the proverbial fashion food chain. "So, you think you are above the decision, but I actually chose your sweater today for you," the editor tells Andy.

While any decent gal reads this passage with sympathy for Andy and thinks, "Get over yourself, editor…it's a blouse," the editor character actually has a point: we're all connected, and even a highly personal decision like which clothes to wear today is influenced by a long, invisible chain of decisions made by the people around us. The editor's words aren't just a rebuke, but a challenge: start paying attention to these connections, instead of thinking she's above them, because understanding how we're all connected will make Andy a better observer and decision-maker. Her point is the same for money. We can think we are above it. We can think that big business, whether it's fashion or banks, doesn't matter to us on Main Street. But the reality is we are all connected, and affected, by money.

What I love about this scene is that is reminds me of the important economic concept of fungibility. (Yes, we can draw smart takeaways from our favorite chic lit books!) Fungibility can be defined as interchangeability. For example, the dollar you give me is no different in value than a dollar I give someone else. Or, the choice of cerulean blue, whether for a $1000 couture sweater or a mass-market $19.99 sweater, is the same. To the editor's point, Andy's choice of cerulean blue is not really so different from the fashion choices the editor makes—they're all connected by the same fashion economy. Our actions and lives are interconnected in ways we cannot even begin to imagine.

Spend a dollar today on your girls' weekend in South Beach and see it end up in the college savings jar of a teenager in Brazil. Throw a fun wedding and you may help pay for someone else's. Eat out at a nice restaurant and you'll help another family put food on their own table. Nowhere in today's world is the concept of fungibility more obvious or more important than in the financial markets. While much has been made of the Wall Street verses Main Street argument, the reality is that the decisions of one "street" deeply impact the decisions of the other. Two of the places we see this play out are in monetary policy and the regulation of our financial markets.

Unraveling the Blue Sweater

Let's face it, monetary policy seems boring, complicated, and remote. A lot of people don't follow the latest stories about it because it seems hard to understand, and anyway we don't feel like the ups and downs of big banks mean all that much to us in our day-to-day lives. In other words, we're like Andy scoffing at the blue sweater. But monetary policy, once you really understand it, is not only fascinating—it has a big, important role in everyone's lives, especially the growing ranks of women starting small businesses or climbing the corporate ladder. So, how does it all work?

Monetary policy refers to how much money is floating around in circulation, and the actions and regulations the government enacts to manage it. The amount of money in supply matters because it directly impacts how much (or how little) unemployment, inflation, or price increases occur in our economy. Monetary policy is all about making sure that paycheck makes it to your purse, and that it's actually worth something once it gets there. Too much money floating around unnecessarily drives up the cost of items (inflation), and too little money in our system makes it really hard to get ahead despite holding down two jobs and getting free childcare from Grandma.

Why not just have the US Treasury print more money when we, as a nation, need it? Inflation, or too much money in the system, means quite simply that a single dollar is worth less; this occurs when economic growth slows or stagnates but people continue to buy the things they want and need. This drives the price of items up, while the value of a single dollar drops, making things more expensive. To get a picture of an extreme example of inflation, think of the 1972 film *Cabaret*, which is set in the later days of Germany's Weinmar Republic. Liza Minnelli and Michael York aren't just broke because they're free spirited artists; everyone's broke, because the national currency of the Weinmar Republic had become virtually worthless after 1923 due to inflation and poorly managed monetary policy. The result? Shelves went bare in local shops, the cost of a loaf of bread soared to millions of marks, and paper money became so worthless that people burned it for warmth or used it to wallpaper their homes.[1] By 1925, Germany's currency had been stabilized, but the consequences of hyperinflation were irreversible. *Cabaret* is set in the late 1920s, after the hyperinflation crisis had blown over, but German society was still reeling. Many people had lost their savings, the economy was still sputtering, hardship had inspired a series of violent protests and strikes throughout the nation, and the chaos created a vacuum for a charismatic but terrible leader to step forward—I think you know the rest of that story. Inflation is no cabaret.

Okay, so we're not worried about spiraling into that level of crisis—yet. What could realistically happen in America today? Well, as a result of inflation, three primary problems can occur:

First, as prices of those goods rise, whatever savings someone has had to date loses value. For instance, in an inflationary economy, the $50,000 a mother had saved toward her child's college tuition starts to lose value and could become worthless if the price of that schooling continues to rise and there is no corresponding growth in economic output for her to earn more (i.e., jobs weren't more plentiful or paying more).

Second, getting a loan as a consumer, whether it be for school tuition, a mortgage, a car, or anything else, becomes more expensive because, given there's more money in the system, interest rates tend to be higher as a way to slow down spending, including spending as an output of borrowing.

Third, it also means that the cost of our government spending, which is in large part financed by borrowing (those government bonds we talked about previously) becomes more expensive. As lenders see that the government needs more money to fund the system, they can charge the government more interest to lend it money. In addition, as those new bonds pay investors higher interest rates in return for their loans, they are more valuable to investors than the old bonds, thus causing a decline in value for existing investors (who might not be so inclined to invest in our government the next time around).

Remember who ultimately pays for out-of-control government spending? Us, the taxpayers. So even the ways in which inflation affects the government's balance sheet ultimately comes around to hit our individual bank accounts, too, when our tax bill comes up.

On the other Essie-manicured hand, too little money in the system means that people become cautious to spend. Thus, businesses have trouble meeting sales objectives, growing, and increasing their workforces. It also means people have difficulty saving and are, therefore, less prepared for the unexpected and the future.

So, just like work-life balance, balancing the right amount of money in our economy is critical to ensure a healthy level of employment and overall economic growth. This pretty gargantuan task falls to the Federal Reserve Bank, lovingly referred to as the Fed. The Fed has a pretty thankless job.

The Fed is actually a system of 12 banks that are, in theory, independent corporations, along with a Board of Governors, which includes the Fed Chairman. The Board of Governors is an independent government agency consisting of seven officials. The nomination of Governors is made by the President and must be confirmed by the Senate but, as an independent government agency, the Board manages its actions on money supply and funding without any obligation to heed the advisement of any elected official. (So instead of being like a boss, the President's relationship to the Board is more like your mom when you go shopping together—"That skirt's too short" may make you think twice, but can't actually stop you from buying it.) The Governors also approve the nomination of each of the 12 Federal Reserve Bank presidents. The Federal Reserve Bank System essentially lends to and borrows from banks in order to keep a balanced money supply in the system.

Banks are legally required to keep a certain amount of money in reserves (meaning they can't spend or lend it in the public market). Typically, they deposit at least part of these funds with the Fed, which is considered the safest place to put money in the world. Banks may also put excess cash with the Fed if it thinks the Fed is paying a good rate to hold or borrow those funds. (Yes, your bank earns interest on its account with the Fed the same way you might earn interest on a savings account.) And, banks may borrow money from the Fed to fund commitments to invest, or to serve clients, or because it's an inexpensive source of capital at that given time (if the Fed is charging low rates for loans). In other words, the Fed borrows money from banks even though the Fed doesn't need that money, and it lends money to banks, which may not need that money to survive but instead just use that money to make investments or operate in the market without having to sell other assets they hold. In these ways, the Fed manages the flow of money in our economy.

As of July 2013, the amount of US currency—cash and coins— in the hands of the public was estimated to be $1.2 trillion dollars. It is also estimated that most of this is held by holders located outside of the US. Where does all this money really come from? We typically get our money by withdrawing cash from the teller machines (ATMs) or by cashing a check made out to us. Where do the banks get their cash?

To meet the demands of their customers, banks get cash from Federal Reserve Banks or, for smaller banks, through correspondent banks, which charge a fee for the service. The larger banks get currency from the Fed and pass it on to the smaller banks. When the public's demand for cash declines—after the holiday season, for example—banks find they have more cash than they need and they deposit the excess at the Fed. Because banks pay the Fed for cash by having their reserve accounts debited, the level of reserves in the nation's banking system drops when the public's demand for cash rises; similarly, the level rises again when the public's demand for cash subsides and banks ship cash back to the Fed.

The amount the Fed charges banks to borrow from it and the amount the Fed pays banks for the money banks place at the Fed is known as the "discount rate." The discount rate is a benchmark for all other rates, the interest rate upon which other interest rates are derived. In that respect, the Fed and its discount rate governs the cost of money in our system for the short-term.

How does the Fed decide the discount rate? It usually manages the appropriate discount rate through Open Market Operations and a series of meetings throughout each year, based on its analysis of economic data about our economy. (Open Market Operations are when the Fed buys and sells securities on the public market— but we'll get more into that later.) While the Fed can change rates at any time, it typically only does so at its meetings in order to provide predictability and stability in the market.

When the Fed thinks there's too much money in the system and prices might be rising too quickly, it raises rates. This makes it more attractive for banks to put their excess reserves with the Fed because the Fed is now paying a higher rate of interest for that money. By raising rates and triggering banks to move funds to the Fed, the Fed is essentially taking money out of the market system. This is considered "tightening." It can also make our currency, the dollar, more valuable relative to other countries' currency.

But, that also means it can be more expensive for foreigners to buy our now-more-costly exported goods. Tightening also makes borrowing money more expensive for people. If borrowing gets too expensive for too long, it can hinder businesses from borrowing money to fund growth, and hinder people from borrowing money to buy houses and cars, which might make the economic system weak. So all of this is a delicate balance—fighting inflation (too much money in the system) without tightening or slowing the economy too much.

When the Fed thinks the economy needs money or growth, it can lower rates. This action means banks will borrow more of this cheaper money from the Fed, putting more money back into the system (because the money banks borrow from the Fed turns into the loans those banks make to us). That means capital becomes cheaper and generally more free-flowing for businesses and individuals to access. But, if rates stay low too long, too much money can flood the system and inflation in the form of price increases can happen.

For example, let's suppose you want to open an organic cookie shop in your town. You raise some money from friends and family, rent a space, create some marketing materials and a logo, purchase equipment, hire staff, and open shop. In no time, Martha (yes, Stewart) is begging for your recipe and Giada stops by for a visit. You decide to open two more shops in similar neighborhoods and go to your bank for a loan to get started. Your ability to receive that loan is based, in part, on your financial performance and potential, and in part on the bank's tolerance for lending to businesses like yours. The bank's "tolerance for lending" is affected by the bank's lending policies and by the bank's ability to earn money on your loan, as determined by market interest rates. How are those rates set? Say hello to federal policy and Wall Street. That small business loan for the cookie shop is like Andy's blue sweater. Just as Andy learns that the color was "chosen for her" by an invisible chain of decisions around her, even the smallest local business is affected by decisions made at the "Wall Street" level.

In order to afford to loan you the money, your bank, in turn, has to either raise deposits to balance their books against the loan they've made to you, borrow from the Federal Reserve Bank (our centralized banking system), or sell the loan, transferring your debt to another creditor. Banks often sell loans in groups, or pools, to investors who want to earn the interest on the loans and/or who like to bet against the market on how quickly homeowners will repay their loans.

Wall Street firms perform many money-related functions for companies and individuals. But, generally, you can easily simplify what the biggest global banks do. For both their individual customers and their business customers (from small businesses to global corporations to government entities), banks generally provide two key functions: first, providing services to manage money and, second, providing access to money.

For individuals, banks such as Bank of America and Chase offer services to manage your money, including checking and savings accounts and online bill pay, credit and debit cards, and brokerage activities so you can invest in, buy, and sell stocks and other investments to earn income on your current money, under an umbrella we call "retail banking." These banks also offer services to provide you access to more money, generally in the form of loans.

For business clients, banks offer services to help them collect revenues from customers and make payments to run their businesses. Banks also help business customers determine the optimal form of capital to operate and grow their business. (Maybe a company should take a loan from a bank, sell a portion of itself to the public marketplace via a stock offering, or borrow the money from sophisticated bond investors.) Once a company accesses money in the public marketplace, either by issuing stock or bonds, banks maintain a marketplace for those instruments so that investors can continue to manage their holdings in the company by buying or selling the company's capital instruments over time.

What limits banks' ability to make loans to individuals or businesses? Basically, when money gets "stuck" in one place—if people are depositing and saving their money instead of spending or investing it, and/or if investment markets or the Federal Reserve are not lending. These things tend to happen—money gets "stuck" in one place—when the economy is bad. How does Wall Street fit in? "Wall Street," as we tend to use the term, represents investors who lend money to the Treasury by buying bonds. Wall Street is the "money bridge" that connects average Americans with federal monetary policy, allowing economic policies to be implemented. A bond securitization on Wall Street can mean a loan for a new business in Beaconsfield, Iowa, if it influences the availability of money and affordable interest rates in a manner that makes lending and borrowing more possible for everyone. In short, Wall Street enhances the velocity of money in the economy. Wall Street and Main Street are inextricably connected. They need each other like Vivienne Leigh and Clark Gable in *Gone with the Wind*.

Suppose you create the most fabulous high heel shoe ever—think Louboutins with the comfort of Tevas. You find a local designer to turn your vision into a sketch and pattern, and then you identify a local factory to produce a sample of the shoe for you. Perhaps this effort costs $5000. You take your shoes to the nicest local shoe boutique, which promptly orders 50 pairs. They are only willing to pay a bit more than it costs you to produce the shoes, but you use your savings to manufacture the 50 pairs, which sell well. You earn back that personal investment and start looking for ways to grow.

Buoyed by the strong sales, you ship a pair straight to the buyer for Nordstrom's, who thinks your creations are more soothing than a Dashing Diva Spa Pedi. She wants 5000 pairs. Unfortunately, you don't have savings to cover the cost of manufacturing 5000 pairs. You have two options: you can find an investor(s) to give you the funds in exchange for some level of ownership in your company (stock), or you can borrow the money from the bank in exchange for paying an interest rate on the amount borrowed (a loan). There are a variety of considerations to contemplate before choosing the form of money, or capital, best suited for growing your business.

Twelve months later, Nordstrom reorders for 20,000 pairs and Saks calls with an order for 10,000 pairs. While your investors and creditors are strongly supportive, the amount of capital you need for this second expansion exceeds what makes sense to raise from private investors or from your local bank. You seek an investment bank to evaluate the lowest cost of capital (i.e., how to raise the most money for your business while giving up the least, in terms of ownership or interest payments), and they recommend you offer equity (shares, or stock, of ownership). All of a sudden, you are part of the Wall Street financial system.

On the other hand, what happens when the worst comes about, and a business has to close down? Well, this web of interconnectivity protects us too. A business owner can liquidate (sell) her physical assets (things like equipment, inventory, or real estate) to pay back her creditors, and stockholders can choose to sell their shares of ownership whenever they find it advantageous to earn back their investment (or simply cut their losses). We hear about the massively damaging failures of big businesses on the news, but what we don't hear about as often—but is much more common—is a business shutdown that, while painful and difficult, still leaves all parties able to live comfortably and even try again one day. That's possible because the financial and monetary system that connects us all has provided the investment capital from sources equipped to absorb the risks.

Wall Street investment banks and firms facilitate price setting and the flow of capital in markets (by attracting investors and connecting them to businesses) for stock and bonds to flow so that businesses can access the money they need to grow. Like with an individual buying a home, a business must have the track record and cash on hand to justify investors purchasing stock or lending to them via a bond. Otherwise, the risk to the investor is very high that the company will not succeed with its funds.

So why does Wall Street get such a bad name? We tend to associate Wall Street with greed and usurpation—imagine Gordon Gecko from the movie *Wall Street* sneering, "Greed is good." But the truth is, Wall Street is necessary for Main Street to thrive—the two aren't pitted against each other, but intricately entwined and co-dependent. Wall Street is also the bridge that connects federal monetary policy to our everyday lives, allowing the government to enact policies to stabilize the economy and encourage prosperity by maintaining the flow and value of money. If Wall Street enables so many small-town businesses to thrive and so many entrepreneurs' dreams to come true, what's with all the hate?

The Big Bad Wolf

Americans love to root for the little guy, but too often liberals think "rooting for the little guy" means taking the big guys down and printing more money for the little guy to use. When we see extreme wealth and poverty in the world, it's easy to assume that the wealthy are the Goliaths to the poor's David. That's why so many liberal policies are based on leveling outcomes. But in our modern economy, Goliath doesn't have to fall in order for David to succeed. What we really need is a fair field (equal opportunities, not equal outcomes) in which to strive and succeed alongside each other. Liberals' efforts to berate big banks and big corporations are not protecting us women, or any individual citizen for that matter.

Wall Street is a bit like the editor in *The Devil Wears Prada*. It's tempting to pin everything that goes wrong in Andy's life on the editor, but by the end of the story, even though Andy moves on, we realize that she grew from the experience—and that the editor isn't the Big Bad Wolf, but a necessary part of the fashion world who keeps it all going. Okay, we don't end the book loving her, but the important part is that we realize the editor can't be treated as a scapegoat for everything we disliked about Andy's journey through the fashion world—a big part of the problem was Andy's attitude, too (such as her dismissiveness of the significance of a blue sweater).

Blaming Wall Street for everything we dislike about our financial system distorts Wall Street's critical role in some of our country's biggest successes. Plus, Wall Street isn't a single entity, unlike the editor—it's made up of lots of different people and banks, working together. And women make up a small but growing and influential part of the world of "big money," with rising numbers of women entering the world of banking and finance, including venture capital investment,[2] the combustion engine that drives economic innovation.

In such a huge pool of investors and bankers, some of those people might engage in unlawful or unethical practices, and then the opponents of our current system blame the system instead of the individuals. But those bad actors make news because they're the outliers. The successes of the system are so commonplace we might start to take them for granted. While not perfect, the free market system of the United States has yielded unprecedented prosperity for all layers of society. And, its crises have stemmed more from loopholes in legislation than in the freedom of the market itself. Yet much of liberal policy attempts to dismantle the free market system in favor of what liberals consider a more fair and equitable closed system of tight government control.

The problem with our economy is not one of supply or of demand, but of entitlement and dependence. Basically, liberal policy uses the Fed and its monetary policy tools like a big Band-Aid for any perceived economic ills—even if those "ills" are just part of the inevitable ups and downs of business. This over-management and interference is designed to cushion the blow of financial hardship when individuals' and businesses' decisions don't pan out the way they want them to, but their true effect tends to slow economic growth and job creation, and devalue money.

During the Great Recession, the Fed took extraordinary action called Quantitative Easing. Because the discount rate was already essentially zero,[3] and the Fed didn't want to have negative interest rates (that can happen!) it took the unusual action of buying up securities (US Treasury bonds and mortgage securities) to increase competition among investors to buy these assets. That increased the price of these bonds, thus lowering their yield or rate of return, keeping interest rates in the market low. How does this differ from their normal Open Market Operations? Basically, Quantitative Easing is a way to introduce "made-up" money into the system—sort of equivalent to printing more money to make up for a lack of supply. That's similar to what the Weinmar Republic did right before their hyperinflation crisis. As 40% (and counting) of American households are headed by female breadwinners, women have even more reason than ever to be concerned about the value of the dollars they're earning.[4] Our strides in gender parity in the work-force start to lose their sheen when the value of the money that any of us are earning plummets with the rest of the economy.

The Fed is supposed to be non-political and manage in the name of stability and prosperity. However, when any government, including a central bank, intervenes too much in the economic system, it disrupts the natural flow of supply and demand, or market forces, and can actually create significant problems. It is like the traffic light at your Main Street intersection, which works perfectly fine on average days; but on holidays, when the city deploys a traffic guard there to direct traffic flow manually, he doesn't make traffic flow smoother—instead, he causes major back-ups. Markets aren't perfect, but investors are savvy, and when too many controls are exerted over the market, it can suppress market growth and create weaknesses for investors to exploit. One recent example is the Asian financial crisis of the late 1990s, which was triggered by unwise monetary policies that created an infla-tionary bubble in the market, largely centered around real estate, that popped when companies began failing to repay their foreign debts. The crash of the baht (Thailand's currency) set off a chain reaction that affected most of Asia.

In addition to risking an inflationary bubble, when markets get too managed, it tends to lead to over-regulation in an effort to offset the cascading effects of poor policy. This is what happened with Sarbanes-Oxley and Dodd-Frank Acts. Sarbanes-Oxley was passed in 2002 after the Enron and WorldCom scandals (among others) led to cries for increased regulation and monitoring of large institutions active in the financial markets. It enacted a slew of new regulatory requirements and financial reporting require-ments across the business world, as well as imposing criminal penalties for certain kinds of business malpractice. Sounds good, right? No one wants predatory businesses to destroy people's hard-earned savings and get away with it. But Sarbanes-Oxley has a dark side. Five years after the bill was enacted, companies were still seeing double-digit percentage increases in the costs of compliance—the amount of money they spent simply keeping up with the requirements of the law.[5] That means it's just more expensive to run a publicly traded company in the United States—and that means people are either taking their companies private again (buying back shares of ownership) or not starting up businesses in the first place, both of which slow the economy and threaten us with a "tightened" money flow. However, despite all these new regulations designed to protect American consumers and savers, Sarbanes-Oxley didn't manage to prevent the Great Recession.

The Dodd-Frank Act was signed into law in 2010 in response to the Great Recession. A complicated bill, it was the widest-ranging financial reform law passed since the New Deal in the 1930s. In addition to further increasing regulations and oversight of financial and business institutions, Dodd-Frank gave unprecedented powers to the Fed. In addition to piling on more compliance costs for startups and existing businesses, once again making it more expensive and less profitable to operate a business in America, Dodd-Frank also resulted in many changes impacting the average person, such as some small banks ending the practice of offering free checking accounts[6]—which directly impacts average Americans and their access to money and money management services.

Despite how esoteric government money management and Wall Street practices might sound, their actions impact our cost of living and ability to get small business loans, auto loans, and home mortgages, along with a myriad of secondary effects on the job market and the value of our savings. Monetary policy does affect every one of us, whether we realize it or not.

If a policy interrupts the flow of capital that banks facilitate, it disrupts the lifeblood of our economy. It is disrupting the free flow of money between those who need it and those who have it. And, when banks do better and are more profitable, they are better able to extend credit and money to those in need. Being anti-Wall Street is being anti-money. If one thinks Wall Street should be dismantled, she may as well hand all of her money over and say she doesn't care about it and doesn't need it.

It's not just up to the government and banks to make our economic system work. The third piece of the triangle is us, the average consumer. We have to operate with the same integrity, balance, and personal accountability we expect from both of them. So, in that Great Recession, while the banks wrongly created more aggressive securities for investors than were communicated, and the rating agencies shirked their responsibility to appropriately analyze and communicate the risks of those investments, the millions of people who bought homes with borrowed money for which they could not easily pay back are just as guilty. Wall Street makes an attractive scapegoat, and government seems like a tidy remedy, but the truth is, our economy's success is the product of all three parts of the pie (the third part being a wise and financially responsible consumer base). As it turns out, studies are showing that women are better at saving and investing, on average, than men, making important financial contributions to our economy through the power of Wall Street.[7] Women have a lot to gain from a fruitful relationship with "big money"—so taking down Wall Street would also mean tearing down the wise investments of these savvy women.

If we "take down Wall Street," we take down ourselves, and if we blame all of America's recent financial woes on big banks, we won't be talking about, and educating consumers on, the kind of consumer-level decision making that contributed to the crisis, and how to encourage wiser choices on an individual level.

My experience with liberal policies is deeply personal. I encountered many of these regulations when I was winding down my business, Startiste. In fact, it actually took months and months to properly close out all aspects of the business. And, for years afterward, I continued to deal with red tape in order to ensure all "i's" were dotted and "t's" were crossed in terms of our closing. In some ways, closing the business was more complicated than starting it. Closing a business properly in America is expensive, time-consuming, and complicated; if America wants to be the best place to start a business in the world, it also has to be a great place to close one; for, our nation's ability to accept risk and failure and rebirth is at the heart of our greatness.

The Intersection at Wall and Main

If I've got you quaking in your Chinese Laundry wedges, there is hope.

Conservatives tend to prefer less government intervention in monetary policy, which we see as a source of unpredictability and instability. They lean toward a tighter control of money supply, keeping inflation down.[8] One risk of this tight-money policy may be a trend toward higher unemployment rates, but it's a risk that seems worth taking when you consider that the alternative (high inflation, low unemployment) means that the money people *do* earn isn't worth much and savings and wealth creation become near impossible. Conservatives favor individual freedom and choice over government restrictions and regulations, believing that the free market is largely self-correcting—what I came to recognize as "investment in opportunity." A tight-money policy results in more stable markets and a more valuable dollar, conservatives argue, which in turn result in more economic growth, business creation, and jobs. In contrast, many liberal policies on the economy view monetary policy as entirely too slow, focusing instead on tinkering with economic outcomes via fiscal policy (tax and spend), or taking a sledgehammer approach to money creation via Quantitative Easing. Overall, liberals believe that more government control will result in better outcomes for the most people.

The challenge with the liberal view is that, in several thousand years, there remains to be a good example of it working. Socialist-leaning countries like Sweden are often cited for their successful socialism, characterized by high taxes and generous welfare benefits. However, Sweden, for instance, is far from socialist if you look at the market freedoms enjoyed by its citizens, including low regulation, and low incidences of government interference and protectionism. Furthermore, Sweden has a very high labor participation rate, suggesting people work hard for their money. And, for the many services Sweden does provide its citizens, its poverty rate continues to rise. Today, it has a higher poverty rate than the capitalist Switzerland.[9] Most chilling, and proving money isn't everything, every Scandinavian country has a higher suicide rate than the U.S.[10]

The fundamental free market view of conservatives is to work hard; save and spend according to your means, not the means of your neighbors, friends, or the government; and make your own decisions with regard to your lifestyle. Undermining the incentives to work hard, to retain what you've earned, to save for the future and to spend accordingly to your means and wishes is like being married to a tyrannical husband who doles out a weekly allowance for expenses he approves.

History demonstrates that open, free markets enable the most growth and the most financial security for each individual. Understanding how money flows in this country and why a conservative approach to finance policy is critical to ensure one's success are paramount to being a financially savvy, independent woman.

Value Three: Investment in Opportunity

What does an interest rate hike mean for you as you cuddle up in your Lulu Lemons, eat chocolate-covered acai berries, and watch *Scandal*, season one? It means your future. An interest rate hike on the government-set "policy rate" could mean your mortgage rate goes up, the business down the street closes, or the necessities your family purchases every week become more expensive.

When I worked in the White House on China's currency crisis, and then later when I faced massive compliance costs with my own startup, Startiste, I saw first-hand how monetary policy has a highly personal impact on many individual lives and dreams. But even if you're not a business owner or an international policymaker, monetary policy touches your life. It affects your ability to get a car, buy a home, save for retirement, afford the goods you need every day, or enjoy the pleasures you treat yourself to when you have a few extra bucks. All savvy women need to understand where their blue sweater came from—they need to understand how the value of money is set and how it flows through our economy from the huge investment banks down to the corner shop with gluten-free Earl Grey scones.

As a policy expert, I already knew how money connected us all, but my experiences helped me grow in my understanding of the values that drove me—the belief in investing in opportunity, and how important that is for everyone. I realized that investment in opportunity is a fundamentally conservative value. Rather than try to level outcomes for everyone, as liberals do, conservatives focus on growing more opportunities for everyone, so we can all increase our fortunes. The first step is to stop punishing success and stop regulating people out of business.

A lot of people, and particularly liberals, mistake capitalism for a rat race. But once you establish the freedom to earn a living and keep your hard-earned money you can start to explore all the ways that big businesses and small are interconnected. That's why we need policies that allow businesses of all sizes to thrive. That interconnectivity also applies to us and the rest of the world.

Chapter 4

Belief in the Future

We're all connected. We're connected by money (as we've explored in the last few chapters), by family, by safety, by values. Now that we see how the financial fate of the world is deeply intertwined, through investment, debt, and growth, it is worth considering a more primal way in which we're all connected: through the flow of human life, as people (not just their money) move from country to country. Immigration policy is really the bridge between financial policy and security policy, while at the same time being a unique and complex issue in its own right. How it affects each of us, individually, is a highly personal and varied matter. Here's my story.

If I thought managing the debt crises of nations was hard work, I had a big surprise coming when it came to selecting childcare for my family. I've had to muster all my creative problem-solving resources for that one! Finding a legally-documented nanny who drives is like finding a Dairy Queen on an empty stretch of highway six hours into a hungry, ten-hour road trip. (I'm a chocolate cone, chocolate sprinkles gal myself.) I have personally interviewed more than one hundred nanny candidates in a two-year period, only to find three candidates who were willing to work on the books and could produce legal documentation beyond an international driver's license. Take a moment now and log on to care.com. Conduct a nanny or babysitter search in your area, selecting the criteria for willingness to have taxes withheld and ability to drive. See how your results dwindle instantaneously.

What's amazing is how many people will *tell* you that they are in America legally, and that they have a legal driver's license. In many cases, I think they actually believe it. When you question them more about it, they get flustered (of course) but also are genuinely confused. We don't just have an illegal immigration problem; we have an ease of compliance problem. While it doesn't excuse people from making a good faith effort to immigrate legally, the complexity of our immigration laws makes it so confusing that some people sincerely don't understand what their status is or how to correct it. Add in the language barrier and you have a recipe for disaster.

So many people whom I know tell me, "Oh, my nanny is legal. She has a license and drives," when, in fact, their nannies overstayed their visas and have an old international, or even a state, driver's license that they are actually able to renew here—but which does not confer legal residence status. So, think about this: your international driver's license-carrying nanny is driving your kids home from school and gets into a small accident. She is rear-ended as she approaches the main traffic light in town, which causes her to bump into the car in front of her. No one is hurt, but the front car wants to call the police to make a report for their insurance claim. The police come and look at your nanny's license and want to see some paperwork. She can't produce it. They want to bring her in for additional questioning. Your two children are there in the backseat. What happens now, to you, your nanny, and your children?

At one point in my quest for a nanny, my husband asked me what the big hold up was; he didn't understand how I could have interviewed so many people without finding a suitable employee. I must have searched through more than a hundred candidates at this point, just looking for someone who was a legal immigrant and could drive. My husband decided to sit in on a few interviews, just to see what all the fuss was about; he was quickly educated. The next woman we met with offhandedly mentioned bringing her niece over to the United States under squirrely circumstances. While this probably wasn't a great thing to bring up in a job interview anyway, it highlights the casualness with which many people treat immigration law—they often portray it as an annoying obstacle to be got around. However, for those who seek to immigrate legally, it can be more than annoying—it can be a heartbreaking and long-drawn-out process.

So why do people attempt to immigrate to America despite these challenges? Well, because of a value that I share deeply with them: belief in the future. Whether you're born in America or seeking to move here, we all believe in the better future America offers. That's why America is such a desirable destination for so many families, and that's why the people who already live here strive so hard to protect it. Though those two groups may sometimes seem on separate sides of a tug-of-war, they are united by that common value: belief in an American future. I hadn't realized how ingrained that value was in me until I started encountering immigration issues while seeking a nanny. When I encountered a general disregard for immigration law among job candidates and even some of my friends, I wondered why it bugged me so much (besides the obvious fact that I strove to do things above-board). It wasn't because I was *against* immigration. On the contrary, it was because I believed so strongly in the value of immigration and immigrants' belief in the future that I wanted to make sure our laws were respected. I realized that the future we all believed in depended upon a strong and protected America with sensible immigration laws that were respected by all. And the desire to work hard that I saw in these immigrants also made me realize that a belief in the future (for American-born citizens *and* those who came to our shores) goes hand in hand with those same values of financial independence and investment in opportunity that we've already explored.

There's a reason why immigration is an emotional and hotly-contested issue. You'd be hard-pressed to find a person in America today whose life is not personally touched by our immigration system: its history, or its flaws. Illegal immigration is rampant in America and is only one symptom of the issues that plague our very unhealthy immigration system.

Coming to America

America is a land of immigrants. Everyone here comes from somewhere. Sustained by America's promise as a land of opportunity, immigration has always played a significant role in America's history, culture, and economy. While we may associate historic periods of high immigration with Hollywood visions of Ellis Island in the early twentieth century, or the Asian and Spanish influences on California's growth in the nineteenth century, the fact is that America saw a historic high in our immigrant population, at 41.3 million people, as recently as 2013.[1] America also attracts a high proportion of the world's immigrants overall. According to the Pew Research Center, one in five of the world's immigrants has made America their home,[2] making America the world's most popular destination for immigrants.

So, aside from the line we learn in middle school about America being built by immigrants, what's the real story behind American immigration? The twentieth century saw historic highs and lows in immigration, as well as major policy changes, and a massive demographic shift in who was attempting to enter America and make it their home.

Remember Jack, Leonardo DiCaprio's character in *Titanic*? His character is iconic of the last big wave of immigration to the U.S., exactly a century ago. Chances are, you or someone you know is descended from that turn-of-the-twentieth-century wave of immigration, mostly from Europe. Proportional to the existing population, immigrants in 1910 accounted for more than 14 percent of Americans; as of 2013, immigrants account for 13 percent of the American population.[3]

Between these two surges, the proportion of immigrants in the population dropped as America tightened its immigration laws, spurred by war and the economic and security fears it raised in the general public. A series of laws passed between 1917 and 1924 spelled an end to the turn-of-the-century immigration boom.[4] These laws included provisions that sound familiar in the context of today's immigration debate—such as literacy tests—as well as infamous and highly controversial practice of establishing immigration quotas based on nationality of origin. The laws also brought the percentage of immigrants within the U.S. population down pretty steadily for the first half of the twentieth century. It wasn't until 1965's Immigration and Nationality Act, which ended the quota system of the first half of the twentieth century (while not quite eliminating the idea of immigration limits overall), that the trend began to reverse.[5] Just before the act was passed, immigrants made up just 5 percent of the American population. Today, as a percentage of the population, they've reached 1910 levels and, under the current system, are projected to continue rising.[6]

We'd be hard pressed to find an American who doesn't have at least one relative who is a recent immigrant. In my family, my maternal grandfather came from Russia. My paternal grandmother hailed from Paris—she actually came to America with her parents because my great-great-grandfather was a couture designer and sailed over to design for ultra-chic department store Bergdorf Goodman. His wife, my great-great-grandmother, was his muse. Unfortunately, my great-great-grandfather suffered from early eye disease. When he couldn't design anymore, he went to Boston and became an entrepreneur; though, later, he lost much of his wealth in the Depression. His daughter wasn't daunted by his twists of fate, because she became an entrepreneur, inspiring my father to walk in her footsteps. The family who arrived here in the turn-of-the-century immigration boom is still having an effect on me, my family, and our values, today, inspiring us with their hard work, ingenuity, and willingness to take calculated risks. (And, of course, their chic design sensibility!)

So, how do immigrants come to America today?

Current immigration law separates immigrants into several different types, with different privileges and obligations, and requirements for application, associated with each, such as:

- Visitor, student, and work visa holders
- Refugees/asylum seekers
- Permanent residents (green card holders)
- Those who have qualified for citizenship/naturalization

Those four categories just scratch the surface of the complicated system we use to admit people into the United States, but we'll focus on them for now because they are the most relevant classifications for the millions of people who attempt to make America their permanent home. When the word "immigrant" is tossed around on the news, it's often used to refer to some combination of these four groups, plus undocumented immigrants who are attempting to move to America without meeting the requirements for any of them. But in order to make sense of how we got to our current policy stalemate, and how to fix it, we need to start breaking things down more precisely so we know exactly which people and behaviors we're addressing with reforms.

Visitor, student, and work visa holders: These are people who enter with a visa that gives them permission to stay in America *temporarily*. The length and terms of their stay depends on the type of visa they have. For example, someone with a visitor's or tourist visa can only remain in America for a very short time and can't take up any form of employment while they're here. Other visas, such as student or work visas, allow for different durations of stay as well as other terms regarding their permission to work, and their tax obligations. The rules can be staggeringly complex (we'll get into that more later), but the unifying theme is that holders of these types of visas are only supposed to remain in America temporarily—at the end of their visa term, they either have to leave or upgrade.

Refugees/asylum seekers: Certain people from specific regions or demographic groups are permitted entry to the U.S. as refugees, or asylum seekers. Refugee status exists as a humanitarian effort to allow those who are fleeing persecution to seek safety in America—a role that much of the Western world learned to take much more seriously after the Holocaust.[7] However, like the group above, this status is meant to be temporary—after a one-year waiting period, refugees may apply for a green card and upgrade their immigration status to Permanent Resident, which is more desirable for many reasons. People who are already living in the U.S. can also apply for refugee status "defensively" if they are threatened with removal, by demonstrating that being sent back to their country of origin would expose them to persecution either now or in the near future.

Permanent Residents (green card holders): This group frequently gets confused with naturalized American citizens, but there are several significant differences. Permanent Residents—those who hold a coveted "green card"—have permission to live in the U.S. permanently, but they do not have the full rights of citizenship. For example, they can't vote in federal or local elections, they have a much harder time bringing spouses or other family over (whereas full citizenship allows one to sponsor his or her spouse for a green card), they can't hold public office, and they must renew their green card every ten years or face loss of their Permanent Residence status. Additionally, a green card holder may be deported for committing crimes or violating the terms of their immigration status. While these constraints might sound unattractive to those who take the rights and privileges of citizenship for granted, for many families simply attaining a green card is a lifelong dream.

Those who have qualified for citizenship/naturalization: Naturalized citizens are, in the legal sense, virtually identical in rights, privileges, and obligations to American-born citizens. Applicants must already be a permanent resident for at least three to five years, among other eligibility requirements. A variety of special channels are available for children, spouses, those who have resided in America for a long period of time, and other exceptions, though these are generally limited in scope. The application process also includes a test, interviews, and more.

Today, for those who wish to enter America lawfully, there are so many classifications and the process is so confusing, that some people apply for the wrong visa in error, while others may simply neglect to correct their application missteps if doing so is too difficult or frustrating or they feel that no one's going to notice. No matter how you enter, the vast spider web of classifications, rules and procedures would make poor Charlotte's head spin. Just take a look at the State Department's list of visas for various situations—six different visa classifications alone can be issued for "certain family members of U.S. citizens,"[8] which break down even further into subtypes. There are about 100 different visas available for immigrant entry (excluding non-immigrant visas for people such as tourists and diplomats). The variety is astonishing; some classifications vary depending upon the status of the person you're applying in association with (for example, if you are immigrating as the spouse of an immigrant), which means if you don't already know what that person's status is technically supposed to be, you're in the dark about your own, potentially creating a ripple effect of semi-unintentional illegal immigration.

Imagine you're in a family from the Philippines, moving to New York. Assume your parents both got jobs in different fields; they could each apply for different employment visas or apply for spousal visas based on the other person's immigration status, if one of them has a green card. Depending on which visa they choose to base the rest of the family's entry on, your age, your work status, and possibly even where you're from, you could receive one of several different categories of visa for yourself. What if one of your parents loses their job, or their workplace doesn't come through with a sponsorship for their green card or citizenship? You could be back to square one, trying to figure the whole mess out all over again. What if you have to bring your sick grandmother over—how do you determine her status? And how will you navigate all these bogglingly complex rules with limited English skills? Issues like this face the 51 percent of immigrants who are female—more than the female immigrant population of any other nation.[9] As women compose more of America's immigrant population, more and more women will have to deal with the inherent difficulties of our system.

And these complexities also make it difficult for legal citizens who want to help or employ immigrants. Back to my nanny search, I earnestly wanted to give a hand up to a recently-arrived family, but I also wanted to employ someone in a lawful manner. In this way, this kind of situation—where laws are so complex they virtually preclude compliance—encourages casual lawlessness among legal residents as well. Some of my acquaintances were surprised that I was so adamant about finding a legal immigrant to care for my children—that's how commonplace it is to simply regard immigration law as a different category from the laws they naturally assume we all have to follow. That kind of attitude isn't good for *anyone* in society. But I understand where it comes from—law becomes meaningless when it becomes so complex it's nearly impossible to follow.

Some of these layers of complexity started with good intentions. For example, there is a special visa category for "Vietnamese Amerasians"—the children of Vietnamese women and American GIs who served in Vietnam. In 1987, Congress enacted legislation specifically aimed at giving these people special immigration status to the US, so they could be reunited with their fathers.[10] According to the *New York Times*, "more than 21,000, accompanied by more than 55,000 relatives, have moved to the United States under the program."[11] Theirs are sometimes heartwarming, but more often heartbreaking stories, as fewer than five percent are estimated to have found their families. This policy was obviously enacted out of compassion and that same value that unites anyone who cares passionately about immigration, belief in the future—but did it fix anything? It was designed to allow a special class of people who'd been slighted by fate to try to reunite with their families—but instead of making one more highly specific visa classification just for that group, could the same compassion have been extended to thousands or even millions more people around the world by simplifying the U.S. immigration code and making it more accessible to all law-abiding and hardworking people? When faced with so many barriers to full compliance, it's no wonder illegal immigration runs rampant. So, how does someone immigrate illegally? There are several ways people get around the system.

Sneaking in: This is the one many of us think of right away when we hear the phrase, "illegal immigration." Some people try to cross the border illegally by walking into America over an unsecured portion of the border, arriving by boat at an unsecured location, or even hiding in cars or packages while someone else drives them across the border. While a literal dash for the border makes for the most shocking and exciting adventure stories, it's not the only way people get in. This is why simply building a wall wouldn't be an immigration panacea.

Overstaying a visa: A pretty common way people immigrate illegally is simply by violating the terms of their visa, even if that visa was originally acquired legally. For example, they may have entered the U.S. with a visitor's visa, but stayed long past the point at which the visa expired. Or, they may have entered on a student visa and remained long after their degree was complete. There are many different permutations of this technique, ranging from exploiting loopholes in the system to simply hiding out and working under the table after the terms of one's entry have expired.

Entering on fraudulent information: Another method of illegal immigration is to enter America with a visa based on stolen and/or fabricated information, or with a faked document. This is much more difficult to do today thanks to high-tech verification methods, but it's not impossible.

Those are just some of the ways that people enter our country, lawfully and unlawfully. Now that we understand how people immigrant, we have to look at *who* immigrates, in order to reform and update our system.

Who Can That Be Knocking at My Door?

Men at Work sang a great song but they may have not realized what a fundamental question it happens to raise! Who are these people knocking at our door, where are they coming from, and how are they staying?

It is estimated that there were 11.3 million illegal immigrants in America in 2014.[12] That's nearly a quarter of the 42.1 million immigrants estimated to live in the U.S. currently,[13] and 3.5 percent of the total American population.[14]

Today's US immigrant population is comprised largely of Asian and Latin American immigrants. Mexican immigrants are the largest immigrant population in the US, followed by India, China and then the Philippines.[15]

The United States is the most popular destination in the world for would-be migrants.[16] From our economic opportunities to our civil liberties, our country has a lot to offer. And for women, America offers equality and freedom from oppression, perhaps explaining in part why America draws a disproportionately large number of the world's female migrants.[17]

As of 2010, immigrants or their children founded 40 percent of Fortune 500 companies.[18] According to a report by the National Venture Capitalism Association, "Venture-backed publicly traded immigrant-founded companies have a total market capitalization of $900 billion (as of June 2013). If immigrant-founded venture-backed public companies were a country, then the value of its stock exchange would rank 16th in the world, higher than the exchanges of Russia, South Africa, and Taiwan."[19] Immigrants aren't just starting businesses—about 27 percent of doctors and surgeons in America are immigrants.[20] Eighteen percent of America's scientist and engineer workforce is foreign-born.[21] America is also ranked in the top ten nations of the world for economic opportunity for women, ranking number one for parity between men's and women's estimated earned income.[22] No wonder it's a sought-after home for smart, successful women from around the world—making immigration a highly relevant issue for anyone who cares about women's rights.

But this wave of immigration isn't entirely made up of success stories. Some people who come to America's shores can only hope for a better future for their children. While these immigrants struggle, they rely on the kinds of expensive government programs that are already straining our budget—and states, according to the data available, seem to bear the brunt of this burden.[23] It's difficult to create an estimate of the federal and local costs of immigration (both legal and illegal), but key data can be revealing: foreign-born teens and young adults are disproportionately more likely to lack a high school diploma or equivalent (compared to the proportion of the total population that they comprise).[24] Immigrants also comprise a large segment of Limited English Proficiency (LEP)

people: 87 percent.[25] Low education and limited English proficiency are a toxic combination that spells the recipe for poverty
and dependence. Immigration also comes with a security cost:
without the right measures to prevent immigration by terrorist
plotters and criminals, all Americans' lives are put at risk. Just last
year, a woman who emigrated from Pakistan, and her husband,
opened fire at a holiday party in San Bernardino. According to the
FBI, the couple had been plotting the attack since before the wife
even moved to the U.S.[26]

Immigration enforcement cost the U.S. federal government
$18 billion in 2012, making headlines by surpassing the amount
spent on the FBI, the ATF, and the DEA combined,[27] yet still failing
to stem the tide of illegal immigration. Beyond the costs of ineffective enforcement, illegal immigration costs taxpayers through
the strain on existing resources—such as education funding. Plus,
there are "soft costs"—such as the cost of crimes committed by
illegal immigrants. While it's untrue that illegal immigrants (or
immigrants in general) are more likely to commit crimes than
native-born Americans,[28] those crimes are preventable—by better
immigration enforcement.

There are lots of harmless people who earnestly want to work
hard and make a better life for themselves in America, but the
convolution of our current immigration system either prevents
them from immigrating legally, or makes it prohibitively difficult.
In addition to the sad nature of their plight, there's an economic
cost to making it too difficult for well-meaning and hardworking
people to immigrate legally: we are potentially excluding valuable
minds and bodies from our economic system, keeping out people
who may enhance our economy at every level. Yet we have to
balance those concerns with the equally important issues of maintaining physical security (reducing crime and terrorism) and our

financial strength (discouraging dependence on government assistance). So, to start, how do liberals approach the situation?

Home of the Brave, Land of the Freebie?

Liberals have a very attractive and elegantly simple solution: universal amnesty. "Amnesty" means a governmental pardon to a large group of people, but thanks to Amnesty International, many of us tend to associate the word more generally with a sense of humanitarian justice and good-doing. It certainly has a benevolent connotation. And it's staggeringly straightforward and self-explanatory: just give a pardon to all illegal immigrants within a foregoing window of time.

Let's say we gave amnesty to every person who immigrated illegally since 2000. Now what? Do we give each of these people a green card right away? Are they absolved of the crime of entering or staying illegally, but they still have to acquire a visa of some kind to continue staying? Do we have the administrative power to handle that many visa applications all at once? Are we screening them to ensure that people don't use this amnesty to rush the border and then claim they were here all along? Or to ensure that we aren't granting amnesty to someone who was already deported once for criminal behavior? How about people who may have connections to terrorist organizations? Or people who don't have a job and don't plan to get one?

Not only must these questions be addressed in any amnesty bill, they affect far more people than just the immigrants and immigration administrators involved. *Everyone* feels the effects of immigration, whether it's through our safety and security or via our tax bill.

Amnesty doesn't answer the existing problems in our immigration policy. Liberals have yet to explain how we, as a country, pay for it, how we justify turning our country's rule of law on its head without triggering dangerous precedent for disregarding the law, and how we can protect and defend our country in the process from those entering who intend to do harm. While amnesty for certain individuals may be part of the path toward a more sensible immigration policy, it must be accompanied by provisions that address some of American immigration's biggest problems.

Immigration policy is also prey to far too much liberal bureaucratic tinkering at the federal level. To Congress, when all you have is a hammer, everything looks like a nail. So when a humanitarian crisis arises—like the plight of Vietnamese Amerasians who are seeking their families in the U.S.—the obvious solution, for Congress, is to enact another federal law to deal with it. These new laws add to the layers of bureaucracy and expense already involved in administering our immigration code, making it harder still to keep immigration employees trained and up-to-date on the latest provisions. According to the *Wall Street Journal*, "The Obama administration spent more on immigration enforcement in [FY 2012] than on all other federal criminal law enforcement combined," totaling $18 billion.[29] Yet illegal immigration still runs rampant.

Ironically enough, this mess of laws and provisions may make it harder to immigrate legally, but might also make it easier to *stay* illegally, because enforcement of this hugely complex set of laws is so difficult. In 2013, under the Obama administration, the U.S. issued more than nine million nonimmigrant—or temporary— visas for tourists, business travel, and students.[30] Unfortunately, the cold reality is that a good number of those persons overstay their visa duration and remain in the U.S. undocumented. There is one undocumented person for every ten families in America.[31]

Think about that: walk down the street in any major American city, and you are likely to pass an undocumented American.

These stats shouldn't be entirely surprising, because people come to America looking for a better life—and that means many of them start off with significant challenges, like low education and poverty. But, equally, if not more, important is whether they are arriving equipped with the cultural values to assimilate and make a more prosperous, and peaceful, life in American society? Well, part of that depends on the cultures they're coming from. It's the elephant in the room, especially given the darker side of America's old quota system or historic incidents of rejecting refugees. There must be a middle way between turning a blind eye to potential disaster, and shutting the door to those in need, however. Immigration reform can't be successful if we pretend that the values of the people arriving here don't matter.

Liberals have long favored protection of civil liberties. But in today's world, we have to consider the balance of the government infringing on a piece of metadata or conducting surveillance on certain organizations verses the massacre of many people on U.S. territory.[32] A slippery slope? Yes. But, a new and more dangerous world? Even more so. Whether we like it or not, profiling—or using data about a person to predict behavior—is done on us in many aspects of our lives. When we undergo a doctor's exam, the doctor considers our history, our verbal explanation of our ailments, along with a physical exam and perhaps testing to draw a conclusion. Service companies use data about our behavior to design and offer us better products and services. While our civil liberties and freedom must be protected, profiling does not necessarily have to be a dirty word.

Let's be straight: some cultures value equality, respect for individual rights, and civic lawfulness less than we'd like. Some of these cultures include those dominated by the radical forms of Islam that push universal adherence to Sharia law, including the mass oppression of women through child marriage, genital mutilation, lack of education, and other systemic human rights violations. How do we deal with those who wish to bring this way of life with them? Europe has set a chilling example of what occurs when assimilation is brushed aside for policies that allow—and even encourage—immigrants to maintain insular communities within their new host countries. In many Western European countries today, the majority of immigrants are Muslims, and their Europe-born children are becoming radicalized—and capable of traveling to the U.S. visa-free.[33] In 2015 alone, 146 people died in France from a series of terrorist attacks that harried the country all year.[34] Europe's story of immigration and lack of assimilation is a tragedy and a cautionary tale.

What about refugees? This is another category of migrant that has posed a serious threat in Europe, including a string of sexual assaults in Sweden, Germany, and other hotspots for asylum-seekers from Middle Eastern conflict. In FY 2015, nearly 70,000 refugees entered America, 20 percent more than in 2012.[35] Despite the controversy surrounding Syrian refugees, 57 percent of refugees who entered America last year were from Burma, Iraq, and Somalia, though the number of refugees from Syria represents a rapid increase from previous years.[36]

Most of the refugees in America are here due to resettlement. Due to America's geography, we receive very few refugees directly; most often, they flee first to a country geographically closer to the one they are escaping from. Then, the most vulnerable among these refugees are considered for resettlement in a third country.[37] According to the U.S. State Department, "While UNHCR reports that less than 1 percent of all refugees are eventually resettled in third countries, the United States welcomes more than half of these refugees, more than all other resettlement countries combined."[38]

In fact, American admission of refugees has remained high despite public disapproval at times.[39] We want to uphold our place as a humane and compassionate nation, but we must also protect our security; together, these constitute our belief in the future, that America is a place to seek sanctuary, but it can only be that place if we protect ourselves first. The rise of non-state actors—groups such as ISIL that exist outside national boundaries—raise the need to carefully and individually screen all people who seek to enter the U.S. While the U.S. has only taken a little more than 2,000 Syrian refugees, the San Bernardino tragedy has proven it only takes one or two people to cause terrible destruction. Furthermore, our neighbors have been, and plan to be, more open to refugees from war-torn areas like Syria.[40] As a border neighbor, Canada's more lenient refugee policy demonstrates the need for great partnership between our two countries to ensure that the policies of one don't put at risk the security of the other.

What are our alternatives to these failed or failing policies?

Land of the Free

Upholding America's place as a land of opportunity and growth while protecting our security and economy is a delicate balancing act. That's probably why there are so many extreme solutions to the immigration issue on both sides of the aisle—because most of us are attracted to a simple, sweeping answer to a huge and complicated question. The problem is, many of those "answers" are kind of like seeing a patient with a bruise and suggesting an amputation. It doesn't take much research at all to educate ourselves a bit more on the issue and rise above the shouting match.

Universal amnesty isn't a solution; it's just passing the buck to the next administration. It doesn't solve the problems of how to make sure the hardworking people who understand and embrace American values have a welcome in our country, while restricting entry for those who seek to drain our resources or, worse, undermine what America stands for. Thirty percent of immigrants do not have a high school diploma or equivalent, which is higher than the prevailing rate for the native-born population.[41] Twenty-four percent receive public health insurance, and thirty-one percent of children living in poverty in the U.S. have immigrant parents.[42] In order to fulfill the belief in the future that we all share, America must maintain a robust economy, and that includes protecting our resources.

Everyone here is from somewhere else, but the unfortunate reality is that we all fit into a resource equation. Each illegal immigrant adds strain to our resources without paying taxes into the system to offset their costs. The money to pay for those services, such as education funds to support illegal immigrants' children or additional law enforcement funds, comes out of the pockets of other hardworking people, many of whom are struggling just as much (some of whom may be legal immigrants themselves), but are at least operating above board and contributing to the system. America needs an immigration policy that protects current citizens, while providing opportunity for those who arrive at our shores with a dream of self-sufficiency.

Amnesty has its place in immigration reform, even if universal amnesty isn't the answer. After reviewing everything that's wrong with our system, it's clear in some cases why many fail to adhere to a law so complex and confounding that it's virtually impossible to follow. And while breaking a law is breaking a law, we need to deal with the more than 11 million illegal immigrants in a way that is financially feasible and in accordance with our Bill of Rights. Believe it or not, technically, improperly entering the country (on an invalid or falsified visa, or by sneaking in) is a crime, but improperly *remaining* in the country is subject only to civil, not criminal, penalties.[43] This loophole could be widened to grant amnesty to the largely hardworking, peaceable immigrants who overstayed their visas but are otherwise in good standing with the law—perhaps along with a penalty that is commensurate with penalties for like-type civil violations. For instance, this category of immigrants could be held to penalties to account for the back taxes they owe coupled with a dedicated amount of time of community service to discourage dependence on this loophole for future immigrants. Amnesty in this case means a path to be a law-abiding resident, but not a citizen. On both moral grounds and in protection of our rule of law, we cannot grant the full rights of the American people to those who knowingly defy our laws, despite how compelling their stories might be.

During my nanny quest, I received a note from one candidate who felt uncomfortable with the questions I'd asked her about her immigration status, and that of her family and friends. I knew she needed the work, and her refusal to continue in the interview process seemed to represent a huge fear of discovery—she seemed like an honest woman, but her immigration status and any allusions to it filled her with fear. It shouldn't be like this. Even if she or her family had overstayed their visas, perhaps a system that allows them to pay the penalty with a few fees, rather than deportation, to reflect their otherwise good standing with the law, would allow her to finally build the better life she came to America for. And that would give immigration enforcement authorities more bandwidth to focus on the real criminals.

I feel strongly that people need to be held accountable for their actions, but if we don't find a way to deal with those families who have become productive participants in our society, we simply end up continuing to bestow upon them the benefits of residence in America, like access to our schools and medical clinics, without holding them accountable to contribute toward their portion of the costs. We also do nothing to shut down the moral hazard that currently exists for people to illegally enter and/or overstay their visas, fostering a general disregard for the law. Under the current system, the costs to serve these populations continue to climb, our ability to monitor and ensure their adherence with our laws diminishes, and everyone loses. So like it or not, the only way to ensure a financial partnership between America and those who have come here, albeit illicitly, and to put a stop to those doing it in the future is to find the most economical, legally desirable, American way to incorporate them. Because, realistically, sending them home is expensive, difficult to ensure (the government isn't even positive of the number of illegal immigrants here), and potentially damaging to the welfare of the children they brought or had here.

What about the people we *don't* want to stay?

It is time to crack down on immigrants who commit crimes and violate our trust over and over again (unlike the sanctuary cities in California where murders and other violent crimes are regularly committed by people who should have been deported long ago). But there's another way to combat crime that doesn't get a lot of press because too many people are afraid of seeming politically incorrect: revamp immigration policy to ensure we are, at least in part, prioritizing immigration from countries that share some of our key values—countries with low corruption and abundant education. America has a checkered past when it comes to quotas and entry tests; there have been dark periods of American history when these measures were used in ways that enforced racism and xenophobia. However, total blindness to the culture and values of the people crossing our borders isn't the only alternative to the tainted quota systems of the past. Of course, our immigration strategy must also continue to offer a safe haven for those fleeing oppressive regimes. But until we look at our immigration strategy holistically, from daily inflows to crisis management, and until we consider how to measure and enforce that strategy to protect our country from security risks, the systematic breakdown and implications for our country are crushing.

The truth is, we actually *do* continue to weight our immigration on a quota basis, but our current system is outdated and doesn't reflect changes in world demographics and cultural paradigms. We simply can't turn a blind eye to waves of immigration from cultures where equality is disrespected, violence is encouraged, and corruption is a part of regular life. On the other side of the coin, we should do more to enable immigration from places with high standards of education and a respect for lawfulness. Those are the types of immigrants who will also contribute substantially to our economy and, most importantly, to our society.

So how does all this work in action? Our current enforcement system is unwieldy and expensive. Part of streamlining this system must include training in the new programs, for maximum efficiency. This may also include public education efforts, so that those who are attempting to enter can learn how to do so lawfully, avoiding expensive mix-ups that not only cost individuals, but the government. Keep in mind, if we cannot even process and enforce the policies we have in place, new, big-government policies certainly won't help much. The difficulty and tedious nature of our immigration process is widely documented. Yet, with today's tools like biometrics and technology, we can improve and simplify processing, enhance training and tracking, as well as make enforcement far more productive.

Another way to protect our borders is by prioritizing technologies, including biometrics, to construct virtual borders that can actually be tracked and enforced. It's not quite as easy as setting up an E-Z Pass system along our 1,900-mile border with Mexico, but there is an answer, however: building a *virtual* wall. Intelligence, greater cooperation between law enforcement agencies, and more thorough administration can all help prevent the worst elements from entering (or reentering) America without laying a brick on the ground. And we can then return more of the power to track and enforce back to the States, which can tailor efforts to the composition and needs of their immigrant populations.

Finally, we must encourage assimilation by ensuring that all immigrants have a basic understanding of how American democracy works, America's founding principles, and the concept of civic and financial responsibility. We must teach immigrants to fully become Americans, with the same respect for American values, if we are even to have an America to offer them in the future. And, we must ensure that we empower states and local communities to have the necessary resources to help immigrants integrate into daily life in a productive and contributory manner.

Let us remember that we are a country of people from other places. The question is not whether we should have immigration. The question is how to make it a reasonably fair, cost-effective, legal path, which helps to renew our country as the best place to live.

Value Four: Belief in the Future

Current U.S. immigration policy affects your life, whether you're an immigrant yourself or you're looking for a nanny or hoping to retain your primary care physician who's going through the naturalization process. Immigration policy also affects financial and business concerns, from the taxes you pay, to your business's access to international talent. Too many times, people turn away from immigration policy because it's big and complex and they figure, "If I, and all my friends, are already U.S. citizens, it doesn't really affect us." But without strong, sensible immigration policies in place, our life as we know it could be turned upside down.

Immigration reform is more than just a thorny math problem—how to maintain a sustainable population and budget—it's also at the heart of a truly conservative principle: belief in the future. I didn't fully realize this until I began my search for a nanny and witnessed, through correspondence and interviews, the broad array of people and perspectives in our immigration story. Belief in the future means that we create laws that welcome the hardworking and responsible into our borders, because our economy is expansive and growth-oriented—anyone can make their own success in America. It is the natural extension of financial independence and investment in opportunity. If we believe that Americans can and should work hard to build their own prosperity and to invest in growth and opportunity, it makes perfect sense that we believe in a future that holds opportunities for everyone who comes to America with a vision and a willingness to work.

However, belief in the future can only be sustained if we also have the right laws in place to protect American security and America's budget from those who arrive with dependence, exploitation, or violence on the agenda. It this way, it ties us to another conservative value we'll dive into soon: strength. If you're trying to educate yourself on the issues, immigration is the bridge between domestic policy and foreign policy.

Belief in the future is very important for all women, whether we are native-born Americans or immigrants ourselves. Belief in the future fuels our dreams of starting businesses, starting families, making a better life for us and for our families. Behind belief in the future is an indomitable optimism that has defined America. But belief in the future isn't *blind* optimism; it is not simply saying, "Let everyone in and it will all work itself out." It entails working hard to protect America and its borders so that America can continue providing a better future for those who do enter legally and with good intentions.

Chapter 5

Leadership by Example

For better or worse, women have to learn a lot of rules and, thanks to all those rules, we women know a lot about diplomacy. We know not to say anything when we see our boss buy a pregnancy test at the drug store. We know to compliment our assistant on her cute outfit just as the guy from accounting on whom she has a crush walks by. And don't even get us started on Thanksgiving dinner! Women understand *why* the rules are important—they're about much more than superficial decorum, they're about building on what those before us started. Rules enable communities by providing a framework for our interactions and relationships; it takes a village to raise a family, start a business, or keep a neighborhood safe.

Women are blessed with what are often referred to as "soft skills:" that combination of intuition, empathy, and decorum that enables us to process and communicate information in a way that yields the best results from everyone around us. And, importantly, we understand that we can relate and connect without abandoning our principles and strength. Women are famous for our "sixth sense"—our ability to sense when someone's lying, when someone's been in our home, or when someone hasn't done their homework. We use our intuition and our knowledge of the rules (and when to break them) to build our success, security, and happiness. My mom always taught me to make new friends but keep the old. These things are the heart of diplomacy.

Believe me, I understand how remote and confusing the world of international diplomacy seems to a lot of people. As a corporate executive preparing to serve at the White House National Security Council, my only exposure to any sort of National Security organization was the NSA (National Security Agency) depicted in the movies. I had no idea how my experience at the National Security Council would connect back to my expertise in finance and business. But I quickly discovered that our economic relations with other nations, along with our combined prosperity, provide a critical foundation for the world's safety and affluence. Along the way, I learned a lot about those hidden rules of diplomacy, as I worked alongside my colleagues to craft policies that affected American economic relations with nations from Argentina to Iraq and beyond. All the while, the rules of conduct I'd learned as a young woman served me well!

Serving at the White House and in America's largest corporations afforded me the privileged opportunity to observe exemplary leadership examples. It also opened my eyes to how disconnected world leadership can seem from leading our businesses, and how disconnected all of that can seem to be from our everyday lives. And, yet, women employ these types of critical leadership values every day to make not only our own lives better but also to buoy those around us. Before my government service, I'd had training in business leadership, and I'd admired, from afar, the leaders in government who managed to coalesce public support for their ideas, and then marshaled those ideas into action. On a parallel track, I was also learning about the principles of individual responsibility that guided my personal decisions (values like financial independence). But it wasn't until I was there, in the nitty-gritty, that I fully understood how the two could be connected; that leadership required setting an example. In order to be effective, leadership had to connect our personal conduct with our public impact and ability to serve. And in action, good diplomacy was the direct result of that kind of leadership.

One of the most important lessons I experienced during my service was the power of diplomacy in supporting and enhancing world order. I had the honor of witnessing first-hand a legendary example of diplomacy in action: Secretary James Baker. Having the ability to see how Secretary Baker was regarded and revered throughout the world, and what he did to improve the situation in the many foreign relations issues he touched, was a life-changing experience for me. The power of the values held by the hardworking team of diplomats whom Baker led, and the notion of service to our country that they embodied, was extraordinary. Baker visited countries that were crucifying us in the press, at a time when global sentiments about America and American foreign policy were plummeting, and he managed to persuade their leaders to support American interests—because, as he demonstrated to them, they were interests each nation shared. I got to witness the epitome of a diplomat, someone whose abilities and commitment to America were exemplary regardless of one's opinion on policy. What made Secretary Baker's leadership extraordinary was his mix of deep knowledge, his values based on honor and service, and his commitment to continually build relationships that he cultivated over decades. For this, world leaders not only respected and remembered him, but also would do anything for him. He demonstrated a set of values, consistency, and commitment that is all too lacking in many of today's diplomatic efforts.

My time with Secretary Baker not only taught me a lot about global affairs, it helped me understand how such a huge and complex web of international relations affects us in our day-to-day lives back home. Diplomacy basically weaves together the fabric of our reality—our safety and security, the availability of goods, and even who we are and the place we call home. In order to understand how, we have to dive deep into the world of The Rules.

America the Exceptional

Diplomacy is an ancient tradition, but it has a special place in American history because, without it, our nation wouldn't exist.

When we think of the founding of America, we often think immediately of George Washington, the Revolutionary War, and Yorktown. We might also think of the Declaration of Independence, which holds the key to what makes America so special—as much as any decisive battle, international relations enabled the creation of our country. While our first president is most remembered for his battlefield prowess, our third president, Thomas Jefferson, went down in history as a master statesman and diplomat. The reverence they both receive says a lot about the place of diplomacy in American values. Alongside Benjamin Franklin and John Adams, Jefferson served on a diplomatic mission to France that was critical in our budding nation's success. Jefferson then served as Secretary of State before being elected president, a role in which he expanded

American territory, defended American security abroad, and encouraged exploration.

Jefferson saw and interacted with widely disparate parts of the world throughout his life and career; and as an avid reader, with a historic library, he understood the lessons of history. He understood that even with a robust domestic economy and relative geographic safety and stability (America has benefited much, in the way of security, simply by being too inconvenient to invade by other nations), diplomacy is key to any nation's success. But especially America's success. Because, as Jefferson knew, America is exceptional, or, as he expressed it in his writings, "an empire of liberty."[1]

American exceptionalism has been tossed around a lot lately, more times than not with a hint of scorn. According to some, it's an outdated and close-minded idea. But, before we can determine if exceptionalism is passé, we have to understand what it is.

American exceptionalism is the idea that America has a unique role in the world thanks to our status as an experiment in democracy. America was unique among nations, at the time of its founding, for being a recently-created, deliberately planned and structured nation that operated on the principles of individual liberty and self-governance. As the first nation in centuries to be created and run on Classical principles of democratic elections and civil liberties, America was the hot new model wearing these ideas to Fashion Week for the very first time. This novel approach was thanks to an intellectual movement of the eighteenth century called the Enlightenment, which saw a revival of the study and application of ancient Greek and Roman philosophical and political texts, and a shift away from monarchy and theocracy and toward self-governing civil society.

This gave America the opportunity to lead by example and show the world just how a free and civil society operated, not only within our own borders, but also in terms of how we set the standard for international relations. In simpler terms, American exceptionalism boils down to leadership by example—and leadership by example is one of the core components of diplomacy. Throughout history, as America set the example of what a free, prosperous, and self-governing nation chose as its core values, even issues that seemed to be primarily of domestic concern, such as Supreme Court cases determining federal law within our borders, really took on universal significance.

The rest of the world took note, especially as America grew in affluence and influence. Now, America is far from alone as a country prizing civil liberties and self-governance. But does this mean American exceptionalism has expired? Some argue that the idea of America as a leader for the world is chauvinistic at worst, shortsighted at best. Why should we consider ourselves so special, these critics argue, when so many other nations now strive for and uphold the values that made us stand apart earlier in our history? In fact, some argue that the concept of American exceptionalism is offensive in its implication that other cultures may be inferior to our own. But that criticism misunderstands what American exceptionalism is all about. The hairstyles of Jefferson's day haven't persisted, but the importance of leadership by example has.

American exceptionalism isn't about proving that we're number one or that we're better than those from other countries. It's about *striving* to be number one—for freedom, for civil society, for safety, and for prosperity. And it's about understanding how our unique focus on these traits can ripple out to improve the whole world around us. Leadership by example does not mean shouldering everyone else out of the way.

Imagine raising our children to believe that if their classmate is special, that our children are then somehow less special. Instead, wouldn't you rather teach a child that they could be special by helping others around them grow, so everyone can rise together? That's closer to the real idea of American exceptionalism.

Imagine you're in a burning building. You need help. Several firefighters arrive. Each one of them scales the building to rescue you and the other occupants. Each firefighter shows exceptional leadership and bravery. None of them refuse to enter the building on the grounds that, "If I'm not the only one who does good, I'm not exceptional anymore." In fact, they each know that the fact that the whole team goes in together is the most powerful proof that their leadership by example is working; it's not a reason to hold back. In the same way, just because the rest of the world is catching up to American ideals does not mean that America no longer has a special place in the world.

In fact, some of the biggest diplomacy blunders of the last century have come about when America backed down from the theory of exceptionalism, and took a backseat in world affairs. These blunders arose from a combination of isolationism—the belief that as long as America doesn't get too mixed up in other nations' affairs, those other nations won't affect us back at home—and a relinquishment of America's special place as a world leader by example. Isolationism haunts both liberal and conservative positions at times. Take the 1930s. At this time, while trouble fulminated in Europe and Asia, America adhered to a policy of isolationism. America tut-tutted at Japan for invading Northern China, but the lack of action to back up our admonition actually served to further weaken America's reputation, instead of setting us apart as a global power for peace and respectful diplomacy. This spineless attempt at "leading from behind" continued for more than a decade, until the Japanese attack on Pearl Harbor finally made clear the necessity of U.S. involvement in the global conflict—at the cost of many lives.[2] If, in hindsight, U.S. non-involvement in World War II seems like an obvious misstep, what of the U.S. taking a step back on the global stage just as we have reached unprecedented levels of interconnectivity and interdependence?

Good diplomacy isn't just about making friends, nor is it about wading into every conflict or picking fights. Diplomatic leadership requires understanding how foreign conflicts affect us back home *and* how America's actions affect the world. Achieving this involves actively building global relationships, and crafting a clear strategy for America's protection and sustainability, domestically and globally. Leadership, underpinned by diplomacy, is about drawing the line sometimes, and holding it. America must embrace her role as an exceptional nation in order to set an example for the rest of the world, and advance our own interests. Is that really happening today?

Backseat Driver Diplomacy

Who doesn't dream of a peaceful, prosperous world? We want to be friends with our neighbors, and we want to be able to set foot outside our homes confident in the belief that our global neighborhood is a safe place. Liberals think the way to do this is to shake off tradition (which they believe has led to so many wars in the past) and take a "modern" approach to diplomacy—one that rewrites all the rules. Their attitude makes sense, on the surface: after all, those old rules didn't prevent two world wars, did they?

Diplomacy requires a clear strategy, strong global relationships, a thoughtful set of principles that form a strategy or plan, and committed action to execute that strategy. No matter what a leader's intentions, a lack of clear strategy coupled with weak relationships not only leads to inaction but also leaves openings for those eager to exploit our lack of security in order to execute their own destructive plans.

President Obama tried to assert his new rules when he threw tradition to the wind and gave U.K. Prime Minister David Cameron an iPod as a gift during his first state visit. The President meant to indicate he was a new, youthful, and change-oriented leader, but instead he undermined the power of U.S. tradition and standing in the world. For perspective, gifts among Presidents typically have great historical significance. For instance, recall the desk on which the adorable John F. Kennedy Jr. was photographed. This desk, the Resolute desk, was made from the wood of a British ship-wreck discovered by an American whaler. Britain's Queen Victoria gifted it to President Rutherford Hayes as a symbol of Britain and America's long history and partnership, commonly referred to as the "special relationship." Almost every American President since, including President Obama, has used that desk; Kennedy was the one who famously moved it into the Oval Office, where you're most likely to see pictures of it now. The desk was a significant gift and gesture—when the ship it was made from, the H.M.S. *Resolute*, was discovered, America and Britain's relationship was strained. The U.S. made a significant gesture by refitting the ship and sailing it to Britain to present it as a gift of goodwill; when the ship was broken up at the end of its useful lifespan, its use in creating a desk that would become a goodwill gift back to America was a major sign of the enduring friendship between those two nations.[3] It is not the size or scope of the gift, it's the recognition of the history and tradition shared among two parties that forms the foundation, and paves the way, for the on-going relationship. This is why homemade gifts are so much more powerful than those bought at the store.

By throwing tradition to the wind, President Obama may have succeeded in demonstrating his youthful spirit and commitment to change; however, he also showed the leadership and people of Britain our past special relationship meant nothing to him. During the 2003 Iraq invasion and the subsequent surge in 2009, Britain was easily America's most important strategic and combat partner.[4] And while aspects of Britain's diminished influence in Washington during President Obama's term stem from the British Prime Minister's policy decisions, including a smaller defense force and diminished intelligence capabilities, it is clear that Obama's de-prioritization of Britain's importance is in stark contrast to the strong partnership President Ronald Reagan and Prime Minister Margaret Thatcher formed to manage the declining Soviet Union.[5]

How else can expressions of friendship go wrong? Take President Obama's statement during his 2007 campaign in which he promised a strong relationship with the Muslim world:

> The day I'm inaugurated, not only the country looks at itself differently, but the world looks at America differently.... If I'm reaching out to the Muslim world they understand that I've lived in a Muslim country and I may be a Christian, but I also understand their point of view.... I'm intimately concerned with what happens in these countries and the cultures and perspective these folks have. And those are powerful tools for us to be able to reach out to the world...then I think the world will have confidence that I am listening to them and that our future and our security is tied up with our ability to work with other countries in the world that will ultimately makes us safer.[6]

Instead, violence in the Middle East has skyrocketed. Non-state actors (rule breakers) like ISIL (the Islamic State of Iraq and the Levant, also known as ISIS—the Islamic State of Iraq and Syria) have grown faster than a Silicon Valley start-up and are causing terror fears around the globe. Just between 2013 and 2014, the State Department reported a 35 percent increase in terrorist attacks and an 81 percent increase in total fatalities.[7] And it's no big secret that ISIL is a major violator of women's rights, including practices such as marrying off girls at the age of nine, denying education to young women, and complete subjugation to their husband's will.[8] Ignoring ISIL is bad for women everywhere in the world. President Obama's statement of support for the Muslim world doesn't seem to have won many friends in the Middle East—perhaps because, when they aren't coupled with strong leadership, words are just words.

The rules of diplomacy, like those of dating, have evolved to their current state for a reason; throwing them away can cause confusion and conflict as other nations might not be as free-thinking as you are (even if you did pre-load your favorite Taylor Swift playlist on that iPod). When other nations challenge our own way of life, too, we can't just "shake it off." Breaking the rules isn't so fun as soon as they're *your* rules that are being broken. The rules of diplomacy don't just help us put our best foot forward, they also protect us from manipulation and exploitation. We all want a peaceful world, but we can't take shortcuts. Sure, some rules are made to be broken, but in matters of national security and world peace, a functioning world order is critical. When order breaks down, rogue forces emerge, like ISIL, and all rules get thrown out the window, fueling chaos.

For an example of what happens when this approach is not upheld in American diplomacy, take a look at the presidency of Jimmy Carter, whose primary failure was trying to be everything to everyone, instead of focusing on American concerns. His stumbles highlight the necessity of focus and strategic planning in American diplomacy.

Carter's work and legacy stands as a testament to post-presidency career rebuilding. While he's known today as an international philanthropist of renown and respect, his presidency is pretty universally acknowledged to be a low point for American foreign policy, by both liberals and conservatives. The consequences were far-reaching; in the 1970s, Americans felt, up close and personal, the effects of poor diplomacy on life back at home.

Carter's record of diplomacy actually got off to a strong start. Embracing the idea of leadership by example, Carter made human rights a defining part of his policy, even coming down hard on allies if their human rights records were not up to American standards. One of his most lauded contributions to world peace was brokering the Camp David Accord, a pivotal moment in the still-evolving quest for peace between Israel and its neighbors. However, Carter's legacy in the Middle East is also blighted by one of the biggest foreign relations disasters of the second half of the twentieth century: the Iranian hostage crisis.

In 1979, series of diplomatic missteps fed the fire of existing anti-American sentiment in Iran, bubbling over when Iranian revolutionaries besieged the U.S. embassy in Tehran and held more than sixty Americans hostage *for more than a year*. While the situation was complex and fault lay at many different people's feet, President Carter didn't help matters in the lead-up to the event, when he toasted Iran's reviled shah, and then offered sanctuary to that same deposed shah against the advice of the State Department, feeding fears among potential revolutionaries in Iran that Carter would back a coup to reinstate him. In hindsight, Carter's actions, while seemingly fueled by compassion—he refused to turn away a terminally ill man from America, where he wanted to seek treatment—were terribly misled. Carter's directionless decisions on how to respond to the evolving situation in the Middle East fed, rather than dispelled, the worst fears of the violent factions that the U.S. hoped to quell. According to Yale historian Gaddis

Smith, "President Carter inherited an impossible situation—and he and his advisers made the worst of it."[9]

As horrifying as the plight of the hostages was, it's still easy to ask, "But how did President Carter's diplomacy affect us back home?" Well, the Iranian Revolution sparked a gas crisis in 1979 that became infamously iconic of the domestic impact of Carter's presidency. Gas prices skyrocketed, and shortages meant that cars in towns and cities across America lined up for hours at gas stations day after day, desperate to buy gas while it was still available. The gas crisis took its toll on America's entire economy, damaging productivity and pocketbooks. Carter's missteps in the Middle East had become a real and immediate problem for American families, and the women who kept them running.

President Carter's fumbling in the Middle East is widely credited as a major factor in his failure to win reelection. His successor, Ronald Reagan, provides an excellent counterpoint to Carter's wavering and ineffective foreign policy. President Reagan, like Carter, was an advocate for peace, but Reagan's motto was "peace through strength." In a 1964 speech, Reagan said, "There is only one guaranteed way you can have peace—and you can have it in the next second—surrender."[10] This was an obvious jab at the rudderless foreign policy of liberal leadership. His point was that taking the "guaranteed" and fastest way to peace was not necessarily the best way if it allows bad actors to flourish; that there can be compelling reasons to hold the line even while the urge toward peacemaking is strong. Reagan stressed the importance of a structured approach in the same speech: "Admittedly there is a risk in any course we follow other than [surrender], but every lesson in history tells us that the greater risk lies in appeasement, and this is the specter our well-meaning liberal friends refuse to face—that their policy of accommodation is appeasement, and it gives no choice between peace and war, only between fight and surrender."[11]

Unlike President Carter, whose attempts at peace-making often involved disastrous compromises and missteps that allowed bad actors to walk all over America, President Reagan understood that peace is best achieved by holding a firm line on core issues. Regan's chief foreign policy achievement was ending the Cold War with the Soviet Union. This unprecedented era of security also ushered in a rise of prosperity at home, in stark contrast with the Carter years.

President Reagan's famous speech was also a warning about the risks of inaction; liberals are mistaken if they believe that the least risky course is to do nothing and wait to see how things turn out. President Obama's lack of clear strategy with Russia and Syria are contributing to a downward spiral in the Middle East, and destabilization globally. For example, as the U.S. remains "cautiously" neutral, refugees overflow into countries with already weak economies and, in some cases, bring with them security risks which affect not just those nations but our own.

President Obama promised Americans, and the world, a diplomatic effort supported by mutual understanding and action. Yet, his inability to build relationships with allies and adversaries, his lack of a clear strategy, and his wavering, passive inaction have weakened America in the world. Just look at the "reset" with Russia—the controversial move by the Obama Administration to reestablish amicable relations between America and Russia, in the good faith that Russia would uphold America's interests and ideals in their own behavior. Instead, shortly after hitting the reset button, Russia directly violated American trust by continuing to pursue a territorially expansionist policy, including invading the Ukraine and annexing a portion of its land.[12] Yet Hillary Clinton,

Obama's Secretary of State at the time, insisted as recently at 2014 that the reset was "a brilliant stroke,"[13] despite the fact that it was so disastrous that two dozen statesmen from Central and Eastern European nations wrote to President Obama begging him to reconsider it.[14] The Russian Federation doesn't have a great track record on women's rights, either, from employment discrimination to minimal protections against domestic abuse.[15] Unsurprisingly, many of America's potential enemies are also enemies of our values, including equal rights and gender parity.

President Obama's approach to the deteriorating situation in Syria has been similarly rudderless. In an interview with Steve Kroft on *60 Minutes*, President Obama stated "…I've been skeptical from the get go about the notion that we were going to effectively create this proxy army inside of Syria." In response to which, Kroft had to ask: "…If you were skeptical of the program to find and identify, train and equip moderate Syrians, why did you go through with the program?" To send American servicemen and women into combat when one is skeptical that they can accomplish their goals hardly conveys the commitment to action necessary to send a message about what America stands for and what we think of our enemies. It was, thus, no surprise the president's mission yielded little result: Putin's Russia stepped into this vacuum of power, and reportedly bombed pro-American fighters in Syria in one of its first acts as a new player in the Syrian civil war.[16]

The consequences of inaction, inconsistency, and ineffectiveness are far-reaching; not only do we pay the dues today, in the loss of security and lives overseas, but America also pays in reputation. According to a 2015 Pew study on America's global image, only 24 percent of nations surveyed had an unfavorable opinion of America overall—but notable among that minority were Russians, 81 percent of whom reported unfavorable views of the U.S., a massive leap from 2012's 51 percent favorability rating from that same country.[17] In particular, Russians do not rate favorable opinions on America's actions against ISIL—troubling in a potential ally with whom we were supposed to have "reset" our relationship.[18] Another hallmark of the failure of the reset policy is Russians' ratings of President Obama himself—Russians responded by 86 percent that they had no confidence in President Obama's handling of world affairs.[19] Equally troubling is how U.S. ally Israel—which otherwise gave the U.S. a high overall favorability rating of 81 percent—replied that only 49 percent of Israelis had confidence in President Obama's handling of world affairs.[20]

According to the study, another notable nation in which favorable views of America dropped was China—widely regarded as a rising competitor for America's status as a world economic and military leader.[21] Most of the nations surveyed showed that at least half or more of the people in those countries believe that China will overtake the U.S. in superpower status.[22] Younger people also responded in greater proportion that they believed China would overtake the U.S.[23]—these are the future statecraft and business leaders of the world, and they've cast their predictions in favor of U.S. decline. If that's not a wake-up call for American diplomats, I don't know what is.

Walking the Walk

Our own State Department defines diplomacy as "a complex and often challenging practice of fostering relationships around the world in order to resolve issues and advance interests."[24] Based on my experience during service, diplomacy is inextricably linked to leadership. I define leadership as having a clear vision and the ability to inspire others toward that vision. How you craft that vision and inspire others requires great diplomacy—an understanding of others' needs, communication styles, and expectations or "rules." Leadership without diplomacy is like a great pair of legs without your 7 For All Mankind jeans and Jimmy Choo kitten heels.

Serving at the White House and for leaders of Fortune 500 Companies, as well as being an entrepreneur, afforded me the rare good fortune to observe some of the most effective leaders in the world. What I discovered is that leadership is leadership, whether you are leading a small company, an enormous one, the entire U.S. government, or a household. As I learned from the leaders in my life, leadership *by example* is the glue that ties personal values, like financial independence or personal responsibility, to the world around us and the movements we create; discovering this was an "aha!" moment that transformed my own life. The techniques required to lead a major U.S. corporation are not all that different from those needed to manage our daily relationships with our spouses, children, coworkers, and friends. I have learned six lessons from operating at the highest levels of corporate America and the White House that I believe not only form the foundation of diplomacy and a great America, but also have a lot in common with the way savvy women run their lives:

Lesson 1: Leadership Begins with Attitude

Good to Great: Why Some Companies Make the Leap...and Others Don't is widely heralded as one of the most important books on leadership. Author James C. Collins and his research team spent years analyzing what makes companies great. Of the seven key characteristics that are critical for companies to transform from good to great, the first is what Collins calls "Level 5" leadership. Level 5 leaders possess an all-too rare combination of humility and drive, and their drive is focused toward improving the company, rather than themselves.

I saw firsthand how Level 5 leadership works thanks to Secretary Baker, who upheld a sense of respect and humility toward all those around him, coupled with an intense commitment to service on behalf of America. I first glimpsed Secretary Baker's leadership style when I found myself working on Air Force Four. Did you know that Air Force Four is set up like a flying office, complete with printers and copiers (and, thankfully, Klondike Bars)? Of course, that means that even when we're flying somewhere, we don't stop working! In my case, on one trip I worked for about sixteen hours on a plane. Every piece of writing we produced was highly inspected and precisely edited, so I spent a lot of time going back and forth among our small team of policy experts, writing new drafts, refining the language, and more. If regular air travel leaves you in a daze, try diplomacy from a plane!

Secretary Baker saw how hard I was working and invited me to sit down with him for a few minutes. There was no pressure; it wasn't a business meeting. He just wanted to ask me about my background and goals, and how I was finding my time at the White House. From my observation, it was not uncommon for him to reach out to staff members like this, to show his appreciation and acknowledgement of their hard work. We had a very small team, and it was important to him to cultivate a community among us, and know each of us personally. Even when we arrived in some of the countries we visited, he'd check to see if anyone wanted to come with him at dinnertime. He wanted us to observe, experience, and learn. Even though he was a powerful and influential person, he understood it wasn't all about him; he was there to serve a mission, just like the rest of us, and if he wanted to ensure the ongoing diplomatic stability of the U.S., he didn't just have to do his job well—he had to work, for years, to make sure the upcoming class of diplomats and policy-makers understood how it worked, so they too could begin building the decades-long relationships that ensure success as a diplomat. His leadership by example began within his own team, through his personal conduct; it was impossible not to see and acknowledge this personal integrity when you met him. Those values and leadership set the tone for the whole team and led to extraordinary results in our efforts to foster international consensus on Iraq's debt situation. Good leaders don't just share their guidance and management skills—they share their attitude with the rest of the team.

Women understand that intuitively—because, in our families and our friendships, we know that setting a good example challenges those around us to rise to our level. Just as mothers know that telling a child, "Do as I say, and not as I do," isn't an effective way to teach them important lessons, or a young woman who wants to escape an environment of toxic gossip knows she can be the change she's looking for by refusing to gossip herself, effective leaders know that their personal conduct is the foundation of the rest of their actions and decisions. And there's no simpler or more basic way to see that in action than by observing how leaders take care of their teams on a human level.

All-nighters seem to be a hallmark of my time at the White House. It's why one of my enduring impressions of the people I worked with was that of unflagging dedication to service. One night, my boss and I were up until the wee hours, crunching numbers and refining communiqués. At about 3:00 a.m., I realized my boss had not eaten anything for dinner. "You have to eat something," I told him. But he was a meticulously healthy eater and we weren't really sure what the options would be at that hour of the morning in Dubai, where we were. Casting around for something healthy, our gracious hotel produced some beautiful asparagus and a fresh cantaloupe—a unique combination, for which we were profoundly grateful! We took care of each other on these missions—yet another example of the personal integrity among the leaders on our team, who wouldn't lose sight of the human element of their colleagues even while they worked to broker world-changing financial pacts. Witnessing how Secretary Baker and others brought the human element into everything they did was a major turning point for my own understanding of leadership.

Lesson 2: Results Build Relationships and Relationships Build Results

One of the best bosses I ever had—because he held me to incredibly high standards, as well as taught and offered feedback continuously as he went—told me "the first half of most people's career is driven by results and the second half is driven by relationships." While this is a bit black and white, I've found that it is indeed generally true and an important principle of leadership.

The global effort to reduce Iraq's debt was an impressive feat that required very skilled diplomatic leadership. It is unusual to conceive, plan, enact and ratify a policy idea within our country in as little as one year, let alone a policy that required the buy-in of many countries around the world. During this period of the Iraq War, America had very little support from around the world; American allies backed off due to pressure from home as the war waned in popularity. We were left with a small group of allies still actively engaged in the effort: Great Britain, Australia, and the Gulf states (who understood the importance of sustained effort as it affected them closely). At the end of 2003, Iraq's national debt became a most pressing issue.

Secretary Baker went about forming and building consensus among our partners quietly, but with transparency. Press around the globe had been very one-sided about the war in Iraq and he understood that a public meeting would be rejected (or at least highly controversial) in the nations he had to visit. He understood that what was needed then was a quiet diplomatic undertaking to give the leaders of those countries the opportunity to consider, ask questions, and build internal consensus.

Thanks to Secretary Baker's decades of relationship-building and many diplomatic accomplishments, from helping to liberate Kuwait to negotiating the end of the Berlin Wall, Baker was warmly regarded by many of the nations we needed on our side the most. With Baker, we were able to go to France, China, Middle Eastern nations, and other places that had been publicly disdainful of American intervention in Iraq, to make our plea for Iraqi debt relief—and we were received by these nations with open ears and arms. That emphasis on coalition-building, while sticking to our primary objectives, came to fruition when the nations of the Paris Club came together to forgive the vast majority of Iraq's debt, paving the way for economic stability—for banks to open, hospitals to reform, schools to grow—in hopes that even more nations and foreign investors would invest in rebuilding a better, safer Iraq. Secretary Baker's results in the first half of his career led to enduring relationships in the second half that made accomplishments such as this possible.

I used to think relationships were relationships and business was business; that's why I had a reputation for being direct in my interactions. I'm proud of that directness, and it's been praised by many people throughout my career, but from my time in the White House, I realized that all business is personal—that networking for success was built on the same principles that guided my personal relationships. That allowed me to open my eyes to the next big leadership lesson, as I learned to negotiate those relationships and put myself in someone else's shoes:

Lesson 3: Perception is Reality

This same aforementioned terrific boss also shared another important lesson with me: "Perception is reality." During my tenure with him, I had a colleague who complained to him that I wasn't team-oriented in my interactions with her. While I was surprised by her comment, he asked me to make more of an effort to be inclusive, and I did. I invited her to lunch and coffee a few times but was rebuffed. I included her in more updates of my team's work but received little response. I asked my boss for guidance and he explained that many times in life, I might actually be in the right, but if someone believes otherwise, ultimately only I can change her opinion. Perception, he told me, is reality. Then, one day I passed this colleague in the hallway. "Hello," I said with a big smile, as I held the door open for her. She walked right past me without so much as a glance or a thank you for holding the door for her. What she didn't realize is that our boss happened to be walking right behind her and witnessed the whole thing. While I admittedly felt vindicated, his advice continued to be necessary and correct. We can only be our best selves.

If someone doesn't see us as our best selves, only we can help to change that opinion—however frustrating that task may seem at times. That does not mean we should change ourselves; it simply means we need to think more like the other person to craft a more effective means of communicating with one another. I'd thought, previously, that I was setting the example I wanted to set, simply by working hard to be a good, responsible person. It took a culmination of these types of experiences to learn that besides just *being* a responsible person, I had to examine how others might perceive me, and adapt to their perceptions and expectations in order to make a good impression and forge relationships. Companies, and even governments, often use a model of leadership called Situational Leadership. Situational Leadership is predicated on the notions of will (desire) and skill (ability) and advocates that any leader can improve the efficacy of her communication with others if she considers their skill and will before engaging. It may sound like corporate gibberish but it's actually pretty darn effective, from the CEO's office to dealing with boyfriends and even toddlers. The next time someone whom you would like to do something for you is reticent, consider their will and their skill. Is it something they can do well and will feel confident about doing? Is it something they like to do and feel incented to do?

"Perception is reality" is also an important lesson for diplomats: even when bad opinions of America abroad are unfair or unearned, those nation's perception of us is our reality, and we still have a responsibility to not only build, but actively maintain, America's reputation abroad, even when judgments against us feel or seem unfair.

Lesson 4: Doing More Doesn't Always Equal Doing Better

At one point, early in my career, I was eager for a promotion to the next level. I sought out my manager to understand what it would take on my part to be ready, and then I began to take those actions...or so I thought. A few months later, with several large and important projects underway, I was reviewing a proposal with my manager when he found an error in my analysis. "Oh goodness, you are right," I said. "I'll fix that right away."

"That's fine, but it's not like you to make that kind of mistake," he said.

"Yes, I know," I agreed. "I'll fix it now."

What he explained to me in the ensuing conversation was that while everyone makes mistakes, he was concerned I was making them simply because I was taking on so much at work to prove to him I was ready for promotion.

"You know," he explained, "being ready for the next level of leadership is as much about knowing what you can't do or get done, as it is about what you can accomplish. It takes a real leader to understand his or her limits at any given time."

That advice has stayed with me. In today's world, with the 24/7 news cycle, the global nature of business, the opportunities for our children, and more, it is all too easy to get caught up in doing everything…and in doing too much. What gets lost is an appreciation for what we do have, a connection with those around us, and ultimately, even the ability to make room for doing more. Women are famous multi-taskers, but many of us learn the hard way that just because we *can* squeeze one more activity or responsibility in, doesn't mean we *should*. Diplomats and policy-makers face the same dilemma.

President Carter's inability to prioritize during his presidency ultimately led to his undoing. By contrast, President Bush employed a focused agenda—one often criticized, but one that was clear and with a mission. History is already beginning to demonstrate that his focused proposals on health savings accounts, immigration, taxes, and combatting terror are forming the basis for solutions toward which leaders today on both sides of the aisle are leaning.

Lesson 5: Make New Friends, but Keep the Old

We have my adorable, strong, omnipotent mother to thank for this advice. Clearly, President Obama giving an iPod to Prime Minister Cameron hasn't worked out so well. By not heeding our relationships with our most treasured allies, from Britain to Israel to Australia to Germany, President Obama has undermined our ability to advocate for our interests, as well as those about whom we care, and ultimately undermined our strength in the world.

Strong leadership through diplomacy doesn't mean forcing your way through every confrontation; it requires sensitivity to other cultures, and a working knowledge of their languages and customs. Sometimes strong diplomacy is conflated with the image of the "ugly American"—the loud and brash person who shows up anywhere in the world expecting everyone to speak English, rudely ignoring local customs, and failing to understand others' outrage at their actions. But that's not the real story at all.

In China, I saw another hidden side of diplomacy. It doesn't sound sexy, but it's one of the most important aspects of brokering between nations: communication. In Mandarin, there are different versions of the words for percentages, and for other complex financial concepts we were trying to convey during a series of intra-government negotiations. Of course it would have been easier to deliver our plan in English, depending on other people's willingness to default to *our* language. But that's not how nations build relationships. In order to use the Mandarin language skillfully *and* communicate precisely what we meant to, our team stayed up all night just trying to select the correct words and phrases. Clumsy translations not only would have damaged our ability to communicate precisely what we wanted to; it would have demonstrated disrespect to the people we were trying to communicate with, by implying they weren't worth the time to try and get it right. And, it would have left them in a difficult position of using our terms, rather than theirs, to communicate with their own citizens. What resulted was a diplomatic agreement that not only met America's goals but also to which China could point and feel proud.

This anecdote flies in the face of the "ugly American" stereotype—while our core interests are in protecting our own nation, we're not so close-minded as to believe that everyone else in the world should expertly speak our language or exclusively adhere to our customs. That flexibility is key in both maintaining existing friendships, and making new ones—as any woman would tell you. It's also a core component of leadership; if results lead to relationships, relationships still need to be vigilantly maintained.

Lesson 6: Clear Vision Requires a Clear Plan

Who doesn't love a little sing-along to "I Can See Clearly Now?" Johnny Nash was absolutely right: clear vision is essential. If you don't have it, you are in desperate need of a new pair of Kate Spade sunglasses. A clear vision is not only an idea, but also a sense of how to get it accomplished. It is the crux of leadership. And diplomacy is the catwalk toward that goal—the path that gets us there stylishly and effectively.

Have you ever been in an argument with a friend or loved one, and lost the plot? Maybe it starts with "Where should we go out to eat tonight?" but as miscommunications pile on top of each other, and become compounded by indecision, it winds up being a conversation about who flaked on whom five years ago and where you were supposed to go that one time. Meanwhile, it's hours past your regular dinner time and you haven't actually resolved any of the problems of the past *or* made a plan for what to do in the present. Trust me when I say this sort of situation is not unique to personal relationships; it happens on a governmental scale as well.

When it comes to American diplomacy, shepherding more than 200 U.S. government agencies, plus Congress, foreign governments, international finance institutions, and so on, toward developing consensus around a vision and enacting it is no small feat.[25] It is far more complex than a CEO simply setting a directive for her employees to follow. For the government and all its attached entities, the agendas are many and are disparate.

My appreciation for this complexity made me wonder how government leaders can really affect critical change without frittering away all their time and energy on internal coordination. Fortunately, Dr. Condoleezza Rice, the National Security Advisor to President Bush during my service tenure, offered valuable insight. Secretary Rice shared with me that she uses a communications model to ensure she's forging and engaging in the most productive relationships while making and implementing policy. Her model, which considers with whom she needs to consult about an issue, whom she needs to inform, and with whom she needs to act, helps her navigate the complex web of our world, while trying to best ensure all relevant actors are engaged in a way that leads to the best policy outcome.

Consult, Inform, Act. So elegant, so powerful, so Secretary Rice.

Great leaders like Secretary Baker and Secretary Rice understand the history and values that inform our nation's diplomatic objectives, and they know that leadership begins with personal conduct and respect and expands outward. In a practical sense, that also includes strong interdepartmental and global coordination, which is facilitated by a shared vision—one of America's place in the world. These leaders also understand that respect doesn't mean being a pushover, and that sometimes forthrightness is the best way to maintain a relationship.

Sometimes, using diplomacy to strive to please everyone makes things more difficult for us, and causes disappointed expectations among our allies down the line. Serving on Secretary Baker's team during the highly sensitive meetings and negotiations for the Iraqi debt relief plan, I learned that we can't say yes to everyone, even if they are an ally and even if they are offering help, if the strings attached are a bad idea in the long term. Plus, there are nuances in this kind of upper-level diplomacy that one might not necessarily consider. The meetings in which I participated were just one part of a larger strategy being executed by several different departments and agencies acting on behalf of the American government. Sometimes those other departments have a different initiative or program going on with a certain country that may be affected by the decisions made by the department for which I advocated. This highlights the often-overlooked but critically important element of diplomacy: inter-agency coordination. Some deeply embarrassing moments arise when the right hand doesn't know what the left is doing. That meant that in some cases, we did well to take a meeting, even though we knew that the requests made by the other diplomats involved would not pan out in that specific instance, because it shows respect and leadership, and keeps the door open for relations with a nation that is important to us.

As it turns out, having a clear vision and plan is important, whether you're picking a restaurant or crafting international policy.

Six Lessons, One Mission: Peace and Prosperity

The world needs America to lead by example. And, the world needs America to dress its leadership up in diplomacy: strong, James Baker–type diplomacy that respects the rules while remaining steadfast in what we stand for. It is America's ideals, grounded in our Founding Father's foresight, that have helped build and sustain our country. More than citizens of any other wealthy nation, Americans believe we have control of our own destiny, that hard work yields dividends, and that today is a good day[26]—it's the summation of all the other conservative values and beliefs we've already discussed. Early nineteenth century French philosopher Alexis de Tocqueville described it perfectly, saying America is "exceptional," a term we still use to characterize our standing in the world. It is America and her values that also propel the hopes and dreams of many around the world. More people around the world want to migrate to American than anywhere else; 150 million people, actually.[27]

The leadership lessons that guide American diplomacy also demonstrate that we can't put our heads in the sand; we must be proactive about determining our place in the world and how to secure it. We must define how we respond at home and abroad to threats and to successes, instead of passively hoping it all blows over. Strength is the glue that holds together American diplomacy.

Every moment of inaction is a boon to our enemies. Remember the isolationists of the 1930s, or Jimmy Carter in the 1970s. Not only is passivity an ineffective strategy for averting international disaster; it puts America at a disadvantage when we do inevitably join in on world affairs, by making us appear weak, and putting us in a reactive position. Isolationism is a seductive doctrine—there's a reason is appeals to both extremes of the political spectrum. One easy fallacy is that war is expensive, so avoiding war (by staying out of it) must promise domestic economic security. However, over and over again that has proven false. Some of the worst economic crises in recent American history (such as the 1979 gas crisis) coincided with times of diplomatic weakness. Greater security—ensured by strong, proactive diplomacy—often encourages economic growth, just like it had begun to after our debt reduction efforts in Iraq. Keep in mind that, by February 2004, Iraq began awarding international bank licenses for the first time in forty years. And, the Central Bank of Iraq (CBI) committed to a free market economy, announcing, "Effective March 1, interest rates on deposits, loans, credits, securities, and all other domestic financial instruments will be fully determined by market conditions." The CBI also committed to "the complete liberalization of domestic interest rates" as well as plans to "establish deposit insurance to provide additional protection to small and medium sized depositors."[28]

So what kind of example are we setting when we lead? America must strive to be the most free, the most brave, the most willing to stand up for our values, so others will follow. We must also be clear about our limits and uphold them. Conservatives understand that diplomacy has to be responsive without being anchorless. Leading by example is more than being a nice person. It's about making tough calls, having a set of values and sticking with them, and then building consensus around them. The kinds of personal values that resulted in such kindness toward their subordinates did not mean that the diplomats I worked with were pushovers—it simply meant they understood the value of human capital.

Leadership in all areas begins with personal principle and builds outward to the examples we set for our team, our team sets for our department or agency, our department or agency sets for the government overall, and the nation sets for the world. Scandals involving the personal lives of diplomats get a lot of press for good reason: diplomacy is personal. The people we appoint to represent us abroad must distill, in their person and conduct, the very best of what America wants to represent about ourselves to the world. From there, we build outward to demonstrate what we, as a nation, stand for. Conservatives understand that diplomacy takes more than celebrity; it takes integrity. Sometimes a tough stance is what it takes to accomplish a great deal of good. I often think of a conversation I had once with my husband. When we'd argue, earlier in our relationship, I'd often find myself telling him, "That wasn't very nice the way you said that, I wish you would say it like this."

He would reply, "There's a difference between nice guys and good guys." I realized, as our relationship ripened, that it was his core values and how they rippled into his conduct that made him a "good guy," even if occasionally I felt that in our interactions he wasn't being the "nicest" guy. He just wanted to protect his family and do the right thing by people.

I realized that this could be true in diplomacy, as well. To use a very recent example, President Obama is a nice guy, but President Bush is a good guy. President Obama very quickly gained a reputation for being "cool," laid back, and modern in his approach to diplomacy. Yet that "niceness" wound up fueling a series of notable (and sometimes tragic) foreign policy disasters, because it wasn't matched with a core of solid values and firmness when it really mattered. On the other hand, President Bush was infamously unpopular during most of his presidency, due to his foreign policy decisions. He was sometimes viewed as old-fashioned, inflexible, or aggressive. But hindsight (and anyone who actually worked closely with him) has shown that Bush did exhibit the core traits of a "good guy:" he was viewed as inflexible because he refused to back down on key American interests, and the "aggression" of his policy was really just a proactive stance put in stark contrast against the reactive policy of previous presidents. And, his biggest failing may simply be that he is loyal to a fault.

Fortunately, niceness and goodness don't have to be an either/or. President Bush would walk into the White House and treat a security guard the same way he'd treat his staff. He once kindly asked me, "Was it worth it?" in reference to my stepping off the corporate fast track to serve in the government. Here I was in the midst of the greatest privilege God could bestow upon me, other than having children: the privilege to serve our great country. That the leader of the free world would even consider that serving his administration wasn't the greatest privilege was a testament to his humility and his commitment to America's ideals—his Level 5 leadership. He and the First Lady committed to reopen the White House after 9/11, to let people see how things work, because he understood the fact that the government belongs to the citizens and we couldn't afford to give in to fear. Bush also embodied those traits of personal integrity that I saw up close in his diplomat, Secretary Baker. The only place that he didn't appear to be a "nice guy," in addition to being a "good guy," was in the eyes of the press.

Leadership by example requires Americans to embrace leadership in the first place—not apologizing for believing that America is special, but celebrating the fact that America does have an important role as a global force for freedom and human rights. After all, these are the core (and conservative!) values that make up the backbone of our diplomacy; but all too often, at home, the idea of American exceptionalism gets poo-pooed as antiquated and colonialist. However, as we've discovered, when America forsakes our exceptional values and role in the world, bad actors often step up to fill the gap.

Support for American exceptionalism has to begin at home. We should be teaching it in our schools, instead of burying it under the idea of multiculturalism. American exceptionalism can coexist with a rich understanding and respect for the diverse cultures of the world. It is only if every generation has a thorough understanding of American exceptionalism that we can hold our diplomats to its standard.

Value Five: Leadership by Example

Women are thoughtful people, detail people, and we understand that accomplishing the most good is not just about pleasing everyone. As a mother, I've had volumes of those experiences, where I've had to explain to a complaining child that I'm not just giving them a gross snack, I'm giving them a healthy snack—and helping them establish healthy patterns that will last a lifetime. Anyone who has dealt with a tantrum knows exactly what I'm talking about. While it might sound reductive to compare international relations to toddler behavior management, the truth is there are certain things about human nature that are pretty universal.

Women do so many things, in their homes and communities, that go unnoticed or unremarked, but we do them because they create a set of values and connections, a bond that lasts. And, we understand that the rules of engagement can matter. Did some well-intentioned friend ever recommend the book, *The Rules*, to you during some period of dating life struggle? That book has been a lightning rod of controversy lately—some women think it's manipulative, while others swear by it. Most of us were able to see through the hype and get what we needed from it, though, understanding that some rules (not all) aren't meant to be broken. We followed our instincts, and followed (or broke) the rules strategically, based on what our knowledge and intuition told us. Ultimately, we let our conscience guide us, refusing to throw off old friends for a new boyfriend, or to trample another woman's hopes in pursuit of a whim. In other words, the dating rules of engagement are a lot like the rest of our lives—and global diplomacy.

Women are natural leaders, as well. We understand the value of putting our foot down, along with the importance of details and the power of upholding our values, instead of just talking about them. Diplomacy intimately affects us, even if we're not globetrotting businesspeople; it affects our pocketbooks, our pantries, our children's education, and our personal opportunities. Women's communities all over the world are threatened by oppressive regimes that do *not* respect women's rights, health, or safety. America's exceptional role as a world leader can enable us to improve the lot of women worldwide, as well as our own daily existence. It all starts with leadership by example: the value of walking the walk, being the kind of person we believe in, and being unafraid to announce those values to the rest of the world.

For me, it was a long road to realize that leadership could unite the personal values I held dear with the bigger political ideas I wanted to pursue. It sounds obvious now, but it's easy to go through life seeing these two things as parallel goals: to be a good person and to be a successful person. Ultimately, it took a host of great examples in my own life, from the dedicated people I worked with in the White House to the professors and bosses in my business life, and even my husband and mother's advice, to learn how the values that I'd thought were purely personal—things like personal responsibility and financial independence—were actually the core components of successful business and political leadership as well. It wasn't enough simply to be a responsible person and also be a good leader—I had to be a good leader *by being a responsible person*, applying those personal lessons to public life. Those two things in combination became another one of my core values: leadership by example.

More than ever, our safety and our prosperity are connected with that of other nations. Just as Main Street and Wall Street are connected by a fine web of transactions, so is America with the rest of the world. We need to be principled and clear as we make new friends and keep the old. We must consistently abide by these core conservative principles, but also understand the needs and customs of the nations with whom we work, in order to grow our global economy and secure not only our nation, but also our leadership position in the world. But, even diplomacy, as important as it is, doesn't mean much unless it is matched with strength, the topic of the next chapter.

Chapter 6

Strength

Maybe you're familiar with this scenario: a young woman frantically dresses for dinner with her first date in months who actually meets the "cute, doesn't live with his mother, and has a real job" standard. In these times of crisis, every gal needs in her arsenal a go-to piece, like the little black dress, that makes her feel strong and sexy. During college, our staples included "flirt shirts," referring to the scoop neck tee's that somehow made all of us look and feel invincible. Strength and confidence are often traits considered "manly," but women understand them deeply as well—we have to master strength and confidence in order to make our way in the world, whether it's on date night or in the boardroom. We women learn quickly the importance of the emotional and intellectual "staples" that get us through those high-pressure situations.

The wardrobe staple is also an important concept in national security. In the case of national security policy, America's fabulously chic and powerful wardrobe staples consist of five elements that, over time, have been proven to ensure great safety and global influence for Americans: strong military power, intelligence (including counterintelligence), homeland security, economic power, and diplomacy. And, these wardrobe staples not only enhance security, they drive economic impact by creating jobs and growth.

I had a close brush with the very serious realities of national security one infamous September day. While my story is not nearly as harrowing or tragic as many others' that day, being in New York on September 11, 2001, put everything into perspective for me. For the first time, a topic that seemed so remote to my daily life—national security, foreign policy, and military intelligence and strategy—became all too personal for me and millions of other Americans.

It was the most beautiful morning, weather-wise, one could imagine. Blue skies, warm, with just a hint of morning breeze. I had been at the Michael Jackson concert the night before. It was an incredible night, mixing with an inspiring and empowering blend of people from all walks of life and ages, reliving their youth in unity—nothing could be more different from the day that was to follow. That morning, an early doctor's appointment led me to justify jumping into a taxi for work, something I didn't normally do. When I gave the driver my work address, he said, "Sorry but I don't think we can get down there. There was some sort of accident or bomb."

As a typical New Yorker, I was initially fairly dismissive. "Please, sir. I have to get to work, can we see how far down the highway you can get?" But, at our outset, the voices on the radio confirmed the harsh reality that something horrible had happened. With no more information than that, I returned home and turned on the TV only to see the second plane hit and to realize this was hardly an accident.

I instantly feared an event of apocalyptic proportions, my mind running through the worst doomsday possibilities; for many of us, in the chaos and destruction and fear, that day felt like the end of the world. I wondered if similar attacks were looming for the rest of the country, and if anyone was prepared. My thoughts also raced to the personal, immediate details of the situation. My roommate and best friend in the world worked at the same company I did, which was quartered right across the street from the World Trade Center. She had left for work earlier than me. Where was she, and was she okay? What about the rest of my team at work, and our friends across the street?

It's almost impossible to describe the panic and worry that consumed us all as the phone lines jammed and we waited to find out if the ones we loved were safe. My roommate and her boyfriend, now husband, literally bumped into each other as they wandered, dumbfounded, downtown. They walked home together. But other than that, our news of other loved ones was scarce. Phone lines were jammed and cell phones weren't as smart as they are today. I couldn't reach family, even those located outside of New York. So, when my mother finally got through to me around 6pm, I'd barely picked up the phone before our tears began to pour out. I went to bed that night forever changed, all too acutely aware that many people that same night were going to bed without the person they had said goodbye to that morning. How could that be?

That day redefined my personal definition of strength.

I was lucky that day and strove to be a strong and supportive leader for my employees, most of whom at the time were young. But, for years afterward, I secretly suffered from PTSD as every dust cloud or rumbling bus made me fear another attack. I had to find my personal strength—that emotional go-to piece—before I began to understand the importance and true value of national strength. While America's global conflicts and security measures may seem remote, they *do* affect every person on a highly personal level.

All that stuff we read about in the daily news—economics, jobs, creating a free world and a free market where we can all thrive and have happy lives—falls apart unless we're also willing to talk about how to protect our freedom and our prosperity from those who'd like to destroy it.

Today's global conflicts are a confusing morass of shifting priorities and allegiances that can baffle the best newsreader among us. In order to understand how American strength comes into play, it seems like we'd need a Ph.D. in modern history, economics, and geography. The short version is: many of today's conflicts are the continuing reverberations of the massive upheavals of World War II. Our grandmas may have shared stories of working in a military factory, Rosie the Riveter style, but how do these conflicts affect women's lives today?

In addition to the obvious threats to our personal safety, women have a lot of reasons to care about national security. As of 2011, there were more than two hundred thousand women in the U.S. armed forces, totaling about fourteen percent of the active duty force.[1] Women's role in the military, while relegated to support tasks in previous decades, has been rapidly expanding; today, ninety percent of military occupations are open to women.[2] Not planning on joining up anytime in the near future? Well, according to some policy analysts, we might not have a choice. Now that all combat roles are open to women, many people are arguing that women have an equal responsibility to men to sign up for the draft[3]--if their arguments prevail, within our lifetimes women may be required to register for compulsory service just like men do in America when they turn eighteen.

Even for women who don't join the service, America's armed forces and our involvement in security measures abroad affect many women's lives intimately. Deployment affects the thousands of families that departing service members leave behind, sometimes resulting in financial difficulty, behavioral issues for children, or emotional strain for those who wait.[4] Additionally, PTSD and other stress-related disorders can haunt families long after a service member comes home.[5] But even if one doesn't have any family members at all in the service, everyone still feels the personal effects of America's military involvement—in our wallets, via our tax bill. The U.S. military had a budget of more than $800 billion[6] in 2015; don't you want to know that money is being spent wisely?

Security policy isn't just "a guy thing." In fact, women have more reasons than ever to care deeply and educate themselves thoroughly on America's national defense. But, sometimes it's hard to hear the facts and reason over the partisan squabbling that fills the news.

Liberals have long been criticized for weak security policy and, in turn, demonize conservatives for their strong security policy prescriptions. Typically, liberals have defended their weak security policies by claiming strong national security is less important than domestic policy. Yet, now, Democrats attempting to protect their party from charges of weakness are encouraging the Obama administration to make the word "strong" a frequent component of its national security policy communications. Unfortunately, the administration's vague, unfocused policies reflect only weakness, not strength.

Conservative policy recognizes that strength begets influence and influence begets power. Power is important because it enables us to ensure the infrastructure and resources to provide for our families here at home, in addition to the fundamental task of protecting us from physical danger in the form of terrorism and war.

Today's conflicts, and yesterday's, affect every single American—and, arguably, hit women and families in special and significant ways. So how'd it all get started, and how do we ensure American strength is deployed wisely and effectively in our quickly changing world?

More Than Just a Map

The geopolitical world as we know it today was forged by the first and second World Wars. When wading into today's thorny security and international relations issues, it helps to remember that many of the nation-states with which we are familiar and take for granted as settled (especially in the Middle East) were actually carved up in the aftermath of these wars. When we hear about Kurds in Turkey or the Israel-Palestine conflict, Baltic upheavals or Russia creeping into Georgia, what we're really hearing about are the continuing reverberations of these post-war land and power divisions.

Take the Middle East. Up until the World Wars, the Middle East wasn't compartmentalized into nation-states with defined borders as it is today. Much of it was ruled by the Ottoman Empire, a political entity that had existed since the thirteenth century. The Ottoman Empire covered a large swath of land, comprising many different cultural and ethnic groups as well as several religious sects, though it was primarily Muslim. In the aftermath of the World Wars, these lands were divided into more modern nation-states, but sometimes the lines were not drawn along the historical boundaries of these different groups. What resulted in many situations were groupings of ethnic or religious minorities (such as the Kurds in Turkey) under nation-states that were highly likely to oppress them. This essentially laid the tinder for an explosion of resentment and conflict that has continued to smolder for decades—sometimes directed at the Westerners that some of these groups believe "imposed" these divisions upon them.

In Europe, Soviet Russia played an important part in the Allied victory of World War II, but General Patton's warnings that it may not be such a good friend for long went unheard. The Union of Soviet Socialist Republics (USSR) quickly revealed its hunger for land and power, gobbling up many nations that had previously been independent of Russia (the historical nation at its core). After the end of the Cold War and the fall of the USSR, some of these territories once again established their own governments, but modern Russia's recent intrusions into Georgia and the Ukraine reveal that the secession of land is still fresh on Russian President Vladimir Putin's mind.

During the period that the USSR was forged, communism spread to Asia, overtaking China and leading to massive upheaval. The spread of communism through Asia led to conflicts such as the Korean War and the Vietnam War, and continues to reverberate today, in the belligerent posturing of North Korea and in China's influence on the world economy.

The modern state of Israel got its start in the aftermath of World War II as well. The Holocaust drove home the necessity of a Jewish homeland, a concept that had been gaining serious traction since the nineteenth century. In the late 1940s, the Jewish settlers of Israel fought to establish their independence, as Jewish refugees flooded into Israel from the resettlement camps where many of them had been languishing since the liberation of the concentration camps. Israel officially became a recognized nation with the United Nations Resolution 181 (also known at the Partition Resolution).[7]

That, in a nutshell, is how the modern world was made—but how does that affect us now, as Americans and as women?

The continuing turmoil in the Middle East has led to the rise of the terrorist groups that currently seek to bring their grievances to our doorsteps. These are the radical Islamic groups behind the terror of 9/11, and today's major attacks. These groups are significantly different than the state enemies we have previously faced for two reasons: first, they operate across borders, often via technology, earning them the description non-state actors; and second, they subscribe to a belief system that values death over life. It is more than challenging to catch and stop people without borders and who are eager to die.

The geopolitical landscape of the twentieth century also resulted in major trends in immigration, which has become a major security and economic concern for America and many of her allies. America's geography and size may have historically protected us from immediate conflict on our soil, but in our increasingly connected world, nothing can isolate us from the conflicts across the sea. America has also been protected by our reputation—but that only lasts as long as we continue to demonstrate our commitment to security and strength.

In addition to the geopolitical landscape, technology is reshaping our security needs. I call these threats emerging technology threats, or "ETT," because in some way, they are all powered by emerging technology. For instance, cybersecurity threats target everything from our cellphones to our bank accounts to our nation's infrastructure, such as ports and planes; agro-terrorism threats exploit vulnerabilities in our food and water sources; and then there are those emerging technologies, such as drones, that could be capable of everything from impeding air traffic to privacy infringements to much worse. The challenge with the ETT basket is that it is changing every moment. Only the most ambitious and innovative efforts will be able to keep up, let alone overpower, these threats.

In light of these dynamics, what does it mean to be a strong nation? And, how do we best protect ourselves? There are a lot of factors that contribute to the strength of a nation, and the global perception of a nation's strength, including the size of the military, the security of national borders, and defense budget as a percentage of gross domestic product (GDP), to name a few. America has always had a certain aura of perceived strength in the world. But, we mustn't take that strength, or the perception of it, for granted—it has to be sustained with strong policy.

Fighting Guns with Roses

America's shrinking military has been a topic of debate for the last eight years of liberal administration, for good reason.

In 2014, liberal lawmakers proposed cutting the military down to pre-World War II levels.[8] The Army, alone, is looking to cut more than 15 thousand combat positions in the coming financial year.[9] Liberals continually make the argument that America's defense budget still dwarfs that of the rest of the world's—total U.S. spending on defense was greater than the next seven countries combined.[10] Will we really benefit by overcorrecting in the other direction? What's going to replace that strength, in our foreign policy?

The liberal approach can be summed up in one word: appeasement, something we touched on already in the previous chapter. Compared to liberals and their continuous store of olive branches, conservatives look like a bunch of sabre-rattlers; and maybe conservatives don't spend enough time communicating how their goals are still the same as liberals'—a more peaceful and free world. So what *is* so wrong with appeasement?

Appeasement translates into an apologist foreign policy that is characterized by smaller, weaker military, politically motivated drawdowns in conflict areas before the fundamentals show it's a good time for those drawdowns, and a general lack of focus and clear principles in defense strategy. What results are weaker, more dangerous conflict areas (because we never got the job done and instead allow terror to come in and fester), and a weaker America (because we have demonstrated an unwillingness to protect our people and our objectives). Because perception is reality, the perception of America as weaker (due to hasty, ill-conceived drawdowns or rudderless foreign policy) translates to actual weakness.

Too often, liberals forsake the "go-to pieces" in their national security closets; instead of wisely exercising American strength, they pretend that if America puts down her guns, so will her enemies. On top of that, liberals are keen to apologize for, and suppress, the values and principles that define America, for the sake of pleasing foreign countries that seek to destroy us. It's sort of like a woman showing up to a party in clothes she's not confident in, because she doesn't want to intimidate anyone else there or make them feel ugly. But doing so only really hurts herself, and doesn't necessarily make the party a better place to be; a better way to make the women around her feel safe and respected would be to stand up to bullies at the party who make them feel bad, not to forsake her own confidence so others don't feel threatened.

Democrats tried to hijack the conversation on strong foreign policy when they elected President Obama, a candidate who, in 2007, touted a softer but still firm approach to American strength abroad. But President Obama had no previous foreign policy experience, and his lack of clear strategy, utter passivity and multiple missteps have contributed to the rise of ISIL, Russia's increasing influence in the Middle East, and economic disaster in Europe, not to mention a weakening of America.

One obvious and recent example is the drawdown in the Middle East. Even when we've decided to pack up and go home, we must be strategic, and ensure we continue to demonstrate strength. In an uncharacteristic move, the top U.S. military commander in Afghanistan, General John Campbell, spoke out against the President's plan to dramatically draw down troops in that area.[11] His argument was that, with the rise of non-state actors such as ISIL, the currently planned drawdown wouldn't leave enough boots on the ground to ensure effective counter-terrorism operations. ISIL's increasing boldness in attacks such as those on Europe and Africa demonstrate that the problem is *not* under control. According to General Campbell, "The Afghan security forces have repeatedly shown that without key enablers and competent operational-level commanders, they cannot handle the fight alone in this stage of their development."[12]

On the other side of the coin are the consequences of poorly-planned interventionism, such as that seen in the conflict in Libya, a debacle that drew scorn from both the left and the right. Missteps like this can be traced to a lack of clear strategy; when we rush into conflict half-heartedly we not only fail to accomplish our goals, but we also put our servicemen and women in undue danger and we leave ourselves open to more attacks, at home and abroad, when our enemies see we're unwilling to commit the necessary resources to our security and international involvement. In the Libya example, NATO and American forces rushed in to assist the rebels of the Arab Spring against the oppressive regime of dictator

Muammar Gaddafi...except that these rebels themselves apparently may have perpetrated their own gross and pervasive human rights violations.[13] Instead of protecting civilians, the stated goal of the mission, the intervention in Libya (according to one brief from Harvard's Belfer Center for Science and International Affairs), "magnified the conflict's duration about sixfold and its death toll at least sevenfold, while also exacerbating human rights abuses, humanitarian suffering, Islamic radicalism, and weapons proliferation in Libya and its neighbors."[14]

The NATO intervention in Libya is almost universally considered a failure—in fact, a failure so comprehensive, it's already being used as the example of how to do everything wrong in a foreign intervention. It was originally proposed as a limited, humanitarian effort intended to assist in overthrowing an abusive regime so that peaceful protestors could prevail and set up a humanitarian (and pro-Western) government in its place. Instead, the rebels who stepped up to fill the power vacuum were radical Islamists who attacked the American embassy in Benghazi, killing six people (including the U.S. ambassador) and injuring many more on the anniversary of the 9/11 attacks. Who needs enemies, with friends like these?

A lack of clear strategy wasn't the only problem with America's involvement in Libya. The intervention in Libya, it could be argued, also damaged America's reputation for strength in the world. The victims of the Benghazi attack were sitting ducks. Now, as ISIL is rising throughout the Middle East, experts are calling for increased American presence to fight the threat, but the president is reluctant even to call those that we do send over "combat troops."[15] Why are some leaders so reluctant to demonstrate American strength, even when it's so clearly necessary?

Liberals don't always get it wrong when it comes to American strength. In the 1990s, America intervened in Yugoslavia when ethnic tensions (another artifact of the breakup of the Ottoman Empire and the reorganization of nation-states and boundaries following World War II) boiled over into war and the secession of Bosnia and Herzegovina. President Bill Clinton made the decision to take American troops into the region, participating in the United Nations Protection Force, or UNPROFOR. The UNPROFOR was deployed with a mandate to assist in peacekeeping operations, reestablish stability in the region, and put a stop to the horrific crimes against humanity that had swept the new countries.

What sets the U.S. intervention in Bosnia apart from the more recent foray into Libya? First of all, it was a decisive and strategic move. This was, in part, due to the failure of a more piecemeal approach earlier in the conflict—the Clinton administration recognized that swift and decisive force would be necessary to bring an end to the conflict.[16] Coalition forces were in a tight spot: up until that point, generally, they had sought to remain neutral, simply preserving peace and providing humanitarian aid. However, remaining neutral in this situation would have meant allowing a powerful Bosnian-Serb force to effectively "cleanse" several major territories of the minority Muslim populations. In a sickening violation of human rights, the Serbs employed systematic rape as one of their strategies against those communities, meaning that as the war raged on, women suffered particularly horrifically.[17] The policy of neutral non-intervention wasn't helping them much, despite its stated purpose of humanitarian aid, as long as it wasn't actively working to defeat the forces that were inflicting this torture upon women.

Instead of holding the course of defensive aid, the Clinton Administration supported Operation Storm, a "powerful offensive" that reset the territorial balance required for peace talks.[18] Diplomatic efforts lead by Richard Holbrooke completed the effort, finally bringing an end to the conflict. Unlike the intervention in Libya, America was willing to proactively demonstrate strength to put an end to a violent and un-humanitarian regime; ultimately doing as much (or, arguably, more) to protect human rights as the neutral efforts of the peacekeeping force, which were limited to providing aid and defensively protecting vulnerable areas with a token (but insufficient) force.

Strength (as any woman could tell us) is a universal value. Conservatives *and* liberals have both fallen prey to the mistaken belief that America can follow a policy of isolationism and minimal intervention and still maintain the global perception of strength. How can we preserve American strength, using the lessons of the conflicts of the last century, today and in the future?

Putting on Our Power Ensemble

If liberals tend to err on the side of non-intervention and appeasement, conservatives have their own unique foibles when it comes to demonstrating American strength abroad. Neo-conservatives and "hawks" have been accused of being too quick to war, especially after increasing criticism of America's self-appointed role as "the world's policeman." But other conservatives, sometimes hailing from the more libertarian end of the spectrum, argue too strongly against intervention of any kind, a head-in-the-sand approach that ignores how interconnected all the world's security concerns are today.

National security and defense are like wardrobe staples: they make us feel secure in who we are, and they tell the world that we mean business. Wardrobe staples also evolve as trends change and make a statement about what we stand for. A strong nation needs strong defense staples to fit the situations that we face in today's international conflict climate. A strong nation also needs to be flexible, forwarding-thinking, and willing to invest in order to meet the new threats of a changing world, whether it be non-state actors or cyberwar. Do we want to risk our futures and those of our children because we aren't a strong nation?

To keep ourselves and the world safe, we have to show up dressed for success. So let's come back to those five staple elements of America's security wardrobe: diplomacy, strong military power, intelligence (including counterintelligence), homeland security (including research and development in fighting ETT and other emerging threats), and, underpinning it all, economic power.

How can America begin by demonstrating strength through our diplomacy? Stop appeasement now. No more bowing to foreign powers and their demands. America has to stand up for who she is in the world. We must leverage diplomacy in terms of good old-fashioned manners and relationship-building, not in terms of caving in to others' demands. (But you're an expert on that already, after last chapter!) We've seen how appeasement weakens America's leadership in terms of the ideas we stand for, so how does it affect our personal safety and security, as well?

More than anyone, women know how dangerous it can be for America to be an apologist. We are the masters of saying "I'm sorry," long believing that those words convey empathy, understanding, and even a sense of personal responsibility. But instead, those words have weakened women, particularly in the workplace. And now, as more than ever we rise to leadership positions, we are actually specifically trained *not* to always say, "I'm sorry." So much so that there are even apps out to help us stop saying it. The founders of one of those apps, the Just Not Sorry Gmail Plug-in, state the case well: "When someone uses one of these qualifiers, it minimizes others' confidence in their ideas. Whether you're persuading an investor to provide funding, announcing a change in direction to your colleagues, or promoting your services to a client, you are building their confidence in you."[19]

America the apologist is no different. Take the Obama administration's refusal to label The Muslim Brotherhood a terrorist organization, despite their widespread and widely documented support of terrorism, terrorist groups, and the doctrine of jihad against the West.[20] The administration's walking on eggshells even extends to overt acts of violence; the Department of Defense has categorized domestic attacks, such as the 2009 shooting at Fort Hood by radicalized Army major Nidal Hasan, as "workplace violence" despite its obvious ties to terrorist ideology. If we are to assert American strength and get serious about the real threats from radical Islam, we must be willing to call these groups and events for what they are. Delicate wording is just one way in which governments damage their strength through appeasement. Historian and foreign affairs expert Victor Davis Hanson likens this form of appeasement to humoring a bully in the hopes that he'll not only give up his torment, but also even change his mind.[21] Refusing to name these groups, such as radical Islamic jihadists, for what they are does not protect innocent people, nor does it implicate peaceful Muslims.

Appeasement has also been disastrously ineffective at stopping North Korea and Iran from developing their nuclear programs. In 1994, the Agreed Framework brokered by the Clinton administration insisted that North Korea halt the development of nuclear weapons, in exchange for our blessing in constructing several nuclear reactors for energy production.[22] President Obama brokered a similar agreement with Iran in 2015, allowing Iran to continue enriching uranium as long as it was for scientific and energy-production purposes and not weapons development.[23] The issue with both nuclear appeasement deals is that they depend upon two notoriously bad actors to play by the rules and not "cheat." Of course, what's the first thing Iran and North Korea do? They use their new capabilities to begin developing nuclear weapons.[24] The 2015 deal with Iran also gives Iran more than one hundred billion dollars. In return, thus far, Iran has taken US servicemen as hostages for a number of days, and shipped hundreds of pounds of enriched uranium to Russia. This is the same Russia who went against America's interest to sign a 2014 oil deal with Iran that enables Russia to effectively bypass western sanctions.[25] This is the same Russia who continues to negotiate deals with Iran in order to secure a potential pathway for Russia to sell oil in Asia.[26] This is the same Russia who has brazenly defied President Obama's requests in Syria and the Middle East, with Russia's own Prime Minister citing a renewed cold war with the West.[27] Appeasement does the opposite of demonstrating strength; it demonstrates that other nations can walk all over America and American interests. Some groups go as far as to say that appeasement lets bad actors know that terrorism works.[28]

Political historians are already calling President Bill Clinton "the great appeaser"… and not in a good way.[29] It seems this may be President Obama's legacy as well, cementing appeasement as the most characteristic liberal foreign policy of the last thirty years.

In order to show our strength, and to give ourselves options besides appeasement, we must ensure and fund an exceptionally strong baseline military. Sounds pretty straightforward, right? Well, the issue is, often when military spending comes up, some people throw it around as if spending more money on our military equals supporting aggressive and over-interventionist military strategy all over the world (the thinking being more money = more fighting). That is simply not the case. The threats against America are expanding far faster than is our military budget. Non-state actors like ISIL have grown in funding faster than a hot Silicon Valley start-up, yet America continues to talk about cutting back our military spending. China is expanding quickly and expeditiously in the South China Sea, through which more than one trillion dollars in goods pass en route to America.[30] Putin is becoming more and more clear about his expansionist plans. North Korea is building new long-range missiles.[31] Throw in the potential for biological threats like small pox, agro-terrorism threats that put our food supply at risk, or a hacking of our financial system that could bring our economy to its knees, and it is clear we have more protection requirements than ever before.

As commentator Reihan Salam points out, "There is a large and growing gap between what we expect of our military and what it can realistically accomplish, given the resource constraints it faces."[32]

During his presidency, Obama has submitted funding requests that simply don't adequately support the strategy he laid out. Some conservatives haven't helped matters, by calling for less defense spending as a way to put America's budget on a diet, but all these calls for a smaller military ignore the very real and immediate threats we face, and even our current military's needs.[33] American leadership must do the hard bipartisan work to put a strategy and related funding in place or we will not only undermine our existing efforts abroad, but also potentially squander funds through partially baked plans and insufficient investments, opening us up to even more threat vulnerabilities.

The military needs a robust budget simply to maintain peacetime operations; additionally, a substantial sum goes to education and training that enables service members to rejoin civilian life successfully, thus strengthening our economy overall. In 2015, the federal government spent about $600 billion on the military and defense, along with another $250 billion on defense-related activities, such as payments into the Military Retirement Trust. Our defense budget nears $850 billion; in 2014, defense spending was 16 percent of federal spending, and it's expected to continue to drop.[34] U.S. defense spending was 3.4 percent of our GDP in 2014, and the percentage of GDP that America spends on defense has been steadily dropping for the last several years, putting us on track for the smallest percentage of GDP spent on defense since the end of World War II.[35] According to these numbers, U.S. spending on defense, as a percentage of GDP, is already dipping below Cold War levels even as global threats multiply. Keep in mind that it costs the military 1% of GDP just to maintain its current arsenal, before any innovation.[36]

Almost 30 percent of the military's budget goes toward compensation costs of military and related civilian personnel.[37] The combined U.S. Armed Forces comprise nearly 1.1 million enlisted service members, and more than 240 thousand officers on active duty.[38] This represents a general decline since the mid-1980s, despite the widely publicized surge in support for the military following 9/11.[39] Additionally, in recent years the armed forces have faced an alarming shortage of qualified officers: as early as 2007, a memo leaked stressing the need to "aggressively" pursue and incentivize officer retention.[40] Yet in 2015, experts were still concerned about the armed forces' "brain drain."[41] The armed forces need the budget required to attract and retain the best possible talent to become the leaders who will keep us safe at home and abroad.

While it's important to ensure our armed forces and defense budgets are well-funded, these areas are also plagued by waste and abuse. In order to both ensure that America is getting the best protection possible, and that our tax dollars are being well-spent, major efforts must be made to cut down on misspent defense money. Recent reports reveal widespread falsification of spending reports,[42] while there are other, obvious sources of waste sitting right out in the open air, such as funding a study on "bomb-sniffing elephants."[43] The issue of waste is not unique to defense spending; the Government Accountability Office (GOA) found $45 billion wasted just in duplicate government programs.[44] Within that wasteful environment, the Department of Defense paid more than $100 million in unused flight tickets, yet made no attempt to collect the refunds available to them.[45] The GAO also uncovered in an audit that ninety-five Defense Department weapons systems drove a total $295 billion in cost overruns.[46]

Despite reform and innovations, our procurement process and the technology that supports it, along with a heaping of congressional special interests and a long process full of red tape, and a myriad of reporting requirements, leave plenty of room to create more efficiency, both in terms of spending reductions and dollar reallocation.

Where *should* that money be spent? We must create a more fluid, efficient system of expenditures, centered on threat assessment and innovation. We must ensure our intelligence community has a clear focus, meaningful support, and the most innovative tools. We cannot let America's heroes be hung out to dry. We need to put more funds toward the Defense Advanced Research Projects Agency (DARPA), acquisition and procurement, and areas that innovate, and we must determine a better way to coordinate across all levels of government, for everything from intelligence work to disaster recovery.

Intelligence is another core component of America's strength. There's continued talk in policy circles about intelligence reform and there's a lot of media attention given to failed intelligence. Intelligence is a process. It's a bit like getting allergy shots—the doctor who mixes the best and right amount of allergen to inject is going to produce the best results; while the process is scientific, it also relies heavily on individual judgment and context. There is no perfect in science and there is no perfect in intelligence. When it comes to intelligence, we, as Americans, need to have an appetite for the imperfect, just as we have for taking risk and overcoming business failure—traits that have fueled our innovative spirit and success.

Intelligence is not perfect, it can't be perfect as it is based in part on human interaction and we, as women, certainly know how hard it is to be perfect all the time. Intelligence experts Mark Lowenthal and Ronald Marks say it best: Intelligence should be about accuracy and utility for policy makers, even though the answer to both may not be revealed for years or even decades.[47] America cannot legislate an intelligence strategy like we did with the Intelligence Reform and Terrorism Prevention Act (IRTPA) of 2004. Rather, we need intelligence strategy that enables real data gathering, supports our intelligence experts, and invests and utilizes the best technology so that big data becomes smart data, and historical knowledge and critical trends are captured, leveraged, and expanded.

What do we do once we've gathered intelligence? We wisely deploy our force. So, how do we ensure America's physical defense capabilities are also up to snuff?

Today, acquisitions—which includes procuring new weapons and technology, research, and development—accounts for only 20% of our military budget.[48] Besides recruitment and retention,

$63.5 billion of military funds go toward research and development of the new technologies that will keep us safe, and keep our service members out of danger, as well.[49] While this may sound like a lot, think about the number of threats we've discussed that are not traditional troops-and-weapons threats. While Homeland Security, the Department of Agriculture, and Health and Human Services are also all working together and allocating some funding toward related defense costs, it is the Department of Defense's acquisitions investment, and programs like the Defense Advanced Research Projects Agency (DARPA)—responsible for science and technology innovation, with its slim $3 billion budget[50]—that will enable us to innovate ahead of our enemies. In addition, the cost of military hardware is rising, meaning that those acquisitions dollars get us less every year.[51]

Let's take cybersecurity as an example, a key focus of DARPA along with several other federal agencies.[52] Both sides of the aisle agree on funding cybersecurity measures, as the Pentagon assembles what is now called the U.S. Cyber Command.[53] The U.S. government was hit by more than 60 thousand cyber attacks just last year.[54] It's not just confidential government information that's at risk, however; our entire economy is vulnerable to cyber attacks on private businesses and individuals that have the power to drain our bank accounts, disburse our private information, and even shut down our utility systems. Cyber security research and development must be a defense priority in the new world of keyboard warfare. Cyber security will be key in securing America against the threat of non-state actors.

America can use the new world of technological combat to our advantage, too, instead of simply staying on the defense. Technology opens many more doors to intelligence gathering and covert operations that can precisely target our enemies while protecting our service members and innocent civilian lives, at home and abroad. Global conflict will never look the same after Stuxnet, the first weaponized computer virus, was allegedly created by a joint American and Israeli force to substantially disable Iran's nuclear enrichment program, without spilling a drop of blood.[55]

The reality is that the number and types of threats against America have increased exponentially in the past years, particularly as globalism and technology begin to blur borders. Layer in the need for far more efficient and coordinated disaster recovery than we've seen to date for storms, which, while deadly, will pale in comparison should we suffer something like an Electromagnetic Pulse (EMP) attack in which a nuclear device is detonated in the atmosphere and shuts down all systems and infrastructure, resulting in starvation, lack of medicine and, ultimately, the new "Dark Ages."[56]

The needs are almost overwhelming. But, they can be addressed successfully if our leaders exhibit strength of mission and conviction to reform waste and regulatory excess, invest in the appropriate mix of futuristic technologies, support intelligence, and leverage technology to protect service members and civilians. To accomplish this, we'll need clear mandates to improve interagency coordination along with coordination at the federal, state, and local level. And, of course, all of that has to be underpinned not only by a clear mission, but also by a strong economy and best-in-class diplomatic efforts. Elle Woods wasn't so far off when she said to her Harvard Law colleagues in *Legally Blonde*: "It is with passion, courage of conviction, and strong sense of self that we take our next steps into the world, remembering that first impressions are not always correct. You must always have faith in people. And most importantly, you must always have faith in yourself."[57]

Along the way, we must learn to be okay with imperfection. We have more than 150 government agencies that need to coordinate with each other before taking action. When, at the White House, we were working to economically stabilize Iraq, we were doing that by coordinating closely (often daily) with our colleagues at the Departments of Defense, Agriculture, Treasury, Trade, State, and many more. Why all the cooks in the kitchen? Because, before one can stabilize a country economically, it must be stable from a security perspective, and its people must have access to basic food and clean water. Only then can we work to reopen schools, hospitals, and banks, and invest in business and the future.

Think about our own country. In America, the concept of Homeland Security is only fifteen years old, originating with the Department of Homeland Security's (DHS) creation after 9/11. Now the third largest government agency, DHS has, along with other key agencies, been a critical resource, for instance in capturing Osama Bin Laden. However, Rome was not built in a day and many challenges, from terrorism to disaster recovery, still remain. Fifteen years after 9/11 we have still not remedied the inoperability challenge that prevented first responders from different departments—like police and firefighters—to communicate.[58] As far as our efforts abroad are concerned we are less than ten years into helping Iraq rebuild. We have a lot of work to do, but that isn't a reason to stop trying.

Ultimately, our strength as a nation will come from a clear mission and strategy, reduced bureaucracy and regulation, increased investment in the emerging technologies, best-in-class intelligence, and true integration among those focused on the protection, defense, and, if need be, recovery of our country.

Value Six: Strength

Our clothes make a statement about our identity and, whether it should be this way or not, our power. They also make a statement about what we mean to do, whether it's blowing them away at the board meeting or finding our serenity in yoga class. Finally, our wardrobe staples protect us from the elements and prepare us for the activities that are most important to us. A savvy woman wouldn't go without her wardrobe staples; so why does it make sense for a nation to go without its stapes of security and defense?

Strength isn't a masculine trait; women need and use it every day. Strength is women balancing work and home; strength is women caring for their ageing parents; strength is women leading by example every day in their communities for their children. Strength is women no longer apologizing but instead proudly upholding whatever it is we need to do or say. I needed strength to see me through the aftermath of 9/11; later, in my service for the White House, I saw how the strength of service members contributed to American might abroad. That was when I realized that if leadership is what brings my values into practice, strength is what enables them to be effective. The pieces were beginning to fit together, between the things that I valued most that I'd originally thought were only relevant on a personal or domestic level—like personal responsibility—and the huge foreign policy decisions of today. A strong America is one where our personal responsibility and financial independence and all the other principles we live by can be transformed into happiness and prosperity, because our interests are protected, both at home and abroad.

Women are not immune to world warfare; even in the heart of America, our everyday lives are touched by the decisions of generals and intelligence agents—they are what enable us to live our lives and make our plans with a sense of security. Nowadays, foreign threats can be localized here at home, like the 2015 attack in San Bernadino, California, by two ISIL adherents. As women, active in every part of our communities--our schools, religious institutions, businesses, and more--we must be part of our nation's defense strategy as well. If we see something, we must say something. Women's intuition is a valuable form of intel. So we must be informed, aware, and active in the security issues of today.

The nations, and non-state actors, that wish to take us down also tend to have bad records of oppressing and abusing women—in fact, American women's freedom is one of the things that offends them so deeply about our nation. If we don't show our strength abroad, those bad actors will come to us—making national security even more relevant to our daily lives. America's strength abroad is why we can drop our kids off at school or plan a fun evening out with friends without having to fear a bomb or major attack wherever we go. But that isn't necessarily a permanent state of affairs; our safety and security must be continuously defended, and never taken for granted. Women don't have to helplessly wait and hope the men sort it all out, however—like Mulan, we can be self-rescuing princesses, embracing the innate powers of female strength. Some women will join up, while others will defend America from home by lending political support to a strong defense budget and wise research into emerging threats. Whatever we do, we can't afford to think of national defense as a "guy thing." It's an everyone thing.

I had always valued strength, but 9/11 and my time at the White House taught me that strength is indeed a personal value that could inform public policy too. Strength as a value forms so much of the decision-making in our lives overall, whether we realize it or not: the friends we choose to keep, the moments when we stand up for ourselves, the way we choose a partner in life, and the steps we take to keep our family safe. In the same way, America's defense must be a core component of policymaking and budgeting—not an afterthought or a "necessary evil."

America has a lot to protect. If the preceding chapters didn't do a good enough job of describing how interconnected we are with the world, history would do a good job of showing, over and over, how America is required to protect her people, freedoms, and prosperity from threats of violence and conquest. Pretending the bad guys aren't out there won't fix anything. But military strength is only part of the equation necessary to ensure a more secure America. The other part, our final chapter, ties everything together in a more uplifting way: how America's strength can benefit the rest of the world as well.

Chapter 7

Paying it Forward

For many of us smart, successful women, being charitable is an important part of our identity; we want to share our success and help those around us. But when we choose where to invest our time and money to help others, we need to look carefully not only at our consciences, but also at the charity's accounting books. In an ideal world, in which time was not an issue, we would meticulously research the accountability and efficiency in their use of funds of charities that have high rankings. We would also seek out charities that help people help themselves. But even when we're not researching our end-of-year giving, we're giving support to those around us in a myriad of ways, whether it's buying a pair of earrings from a friend who just started a jewelry business, or giving some free career advice to a recent college graduate. Women really do want what's best for everyone, but our actions demonstrate that true charity is enabling others to help themselves.

From my own generous mentors, to my years as a leadership mentor to high school girls, I've learned a lot about giving back. I've seen on a personal level how giving that is designed to empower and enable can make a difference in people's lives, and how the people who benefit from it can then go forth and make a difference in many more people's lives. It's a core principle of my life that I learned to apply to policy as I observed President George W. Bush create the President's Emergency Plan for AIDS Relief (PEPFAR), one of the most lauded AIDS-relief programs in the history of the disease, and quite possibly the policy that has saved more lives than any other.

The creation of PEPFAR gave me a unique insight into the role of foreign aid in America's worldview, but it was only one piece of the puzzle. I came to realize that there were other critical pieces, including free markets and global trade, that could do just as much to lift people out of poverty and spread prosperity and security in the world, ensuring a safer global environment for the United States as well. While these are often put into two policy silos, aid and trade are intimately linked in their ultimate objective: paying it forward, or creating a world in which everyone can lift each other up. But just as we discovered earlier with the social welfare policies of the first chapter, sometimes our sense of charity can get away from us, causing us to support well-intentioned but ultimately ineffective or even counter-productive policies. Global aid and trade must be built upon a rock-solid foundation of measurable results and careful research—just like our own personal giving.

We Didn't Start the Fire

Women certainly don't need someone to explain to us why charity is important, or why we feel drawn to help others. But sometimes, in the context of national policy, it can be hard to draw the connections between our national interest and the welfare of remote countries. Some far-right conservatives even argue that foreign aid isn't a national priority for America—but these are often the same people who think that sticking our heads in the sand will make global conflicts go away, too. Isolationism is about as useful in aid and trade policies as it is in the security arena or diplomacy.

Globalization is not a new concept. China's Emperor Wudi formally established a wide network of trade routes, the Silk Road, as early as 130 B.C., which crossed an enormous swath of territory to connect East and West. As trade developed and mobility advanced, it was only natural that new territory would be explored and markets would emerge. Some of that development has been an organic result of human exploration and individual merchants' quest for better profits, and some has been premeditated as businesses and governments seek new economic opportunities for their communities as a whole.[1]

Aid, trade, and innovation became the driving forces of globalization. Even in our own country's development, aid and trade is a history of exchange, in which aid to America from the outside was essential to the founding of our nation, and our return of that aid was a critical building block of one of our most historic and enduring alliances.

After the Declaration of Independence was signed, sealed, and delivered, things weren't looking too great for the American revolutionaries. Their foundling government was strapped for cash, the military couldn't keep its farmer-soldiers from sneaking back home, and its currency was virtually worthless.[2] In order to succeed both at the war of independence, and the economic struggle for self-sufficiency and prosperity, the new America needed some help. And, in 1778, that help came—from America's first ally, France.[3]

The Treaty of Alliance with France of 1778 promised France's military assistance in the American Revolution, but equally important was the Treaty of Amity and Commerce with France of the same year, which ensured that America's new national economy could flourish through a healthy trade relationship with another major world power.[4]

Six years after America's victory in the Revolutionary War, France became embroiled in its own revolution, and the fledging American government found itself immediately faced with the choice of whether it should (or even could) extend the same diplomatic, military, and economic aid to her ally that France had extended to America. It was a very tricky situation. America didn't want to leave her ally high and dry, and in fact initially it seemed that the French Revolution was built on the very same principles that had fueled America's war for independence, making it seem a natural choice for America to show support. But as the French Revolution raged on, becoming ever more blood-soaked and morally ambiguous, American diplomats realized that support for France in this case may not be a great expression of American values, and could also threaten America's tenuous new trade relationship with Great Britain.[5] America's solution was the Proclamation of Neutrality, recognizing the new state of the French Republic, but stating that France's war was a strictly European affair, and America would not provide war materiel to *either* side of the conflict.[6]

America's historical relationship with France is also a good example of how aid and trade are delicately tied to diplomacy and national security—which begins to illuminate why any robust foreign policy must include global trade agreements and, yes, even foreign aid in its scope. Foreign aid can stabilize insecure regions, build international relationships, enhance the global economy, and protect human rights. Like welfare, foreign aid is for nations in dire straits; global trade is the second half of the equation, "teaching a nation to fish" instead of giving them a fish, so they can continue to build their own prosperity and stability.

Today we can see the same delicate web of connections being woven in our aid to Israel. Aid to Israel is controversial, both in America and abroad. America has given Israel approximately $3.15 billion to be spent on defense per year since 2013, about a third of the total U.S. foreign aid budget—and 20 percent of Israel's defense budget.[7] Some have asked why such an astronomical sum has gone to the defense of another nation, so far away from us. One of the reasons is that Israel is a key ally in the Middle East, yet they face an existential threat from their immediate neighbors. Hamas and other terrorist organizations have made it clear that their objective is not peace, but the complete annihilation of Israel, including the slaughter of all the Jews who live there. Aiding Israel's defense is, in a very real and immediate sense, working to prevent another grievous atrocity on the scale of the Holocaust.

In addition, Israel is a valuable proponent of Western values, such as freedom of expression, in the region. Israelis have high favorability ratings of America (81 percent), and are the only Middle Eastern nation polled to express pro-American sentiment from more than 39 percent of their population. Even when Israel's opinions on America are divided between Israeli Jews and Israeli Arabs, Israeli Arabs still give a higher favorability rating to America than surrounding Muslim-majority nations (48 percent).[8] America's support of the Israel Defense Force is also part of a bigger agreement to exchange military intelligence, research, and development between the two nations, so America can benefit from Israel's advancement in military technology—the same kind of thinking that led to breakthroughs such as the Stuxnet virus.[9]

In the same Pew opinion poll, Israel also led the region in support of U.S. actions against ISIL. Now we can start to see how America and Israel's relationship can affect our security, even back home.

Israel is also an important trade partner. America is the largest single trade partner of Israel,[10] with trade between the nations totaling $45 billion in 2012, including $4.1 billion of U.S. exports.[11] And, Israel is a critical brain trust, participating in several cultural and scientific exchanges with America.[12]

That's just one example of how foreign aid and trade is both a charitable act of goodwill and an important part of protecting American interests abroad. America has aid and/or trade programs in place on every continent in the world—even Antarctica, where "aid" consists of our support for scientific programs and the international exchange of knowledge![13]

But globalization, and the need for aid and trade, have pitfalls and can go very wrong. The notion of income inequality fueled by globalization is not only a hot button in our own country but also around the world. It is true that of the thirty-four Organization for Economic Cooperation (OECD) countries, all but a few have experienced rising income inequality.[14] Yet, global poverty is declining faster than ever before. While two billion people were living on less than $1.90/day (the poverty level defined by the World Bank), that number dropped to one billion by 2012.[15] It is critical all countries work to support what I like to call "good globalization," an advancement on behalf of humanity that does more good than bad. Both liberals and conservatives are prone to some big misconceptions about America's relationship with the rest of the world economy, or the best approach to helping others up, even though we're united by the common goal of making the world a better place.

Give a (Wo)Man a Fish, and Another Fish, and Another Fish...

It's hard to say "no" to sending more aid to people who desperately need it, especially when other major civilized powers pressure America to meet the contribution goals they've set for us. (And you thought it was hard to say "no" to giving one dollar at the grocery store checkout aisle!) That describes one of the predominant liberal approaches to foreign aid: run with the pack, and give when told to give. The truth is, without a clear global strategy and strong accountability, liberals' approach to foreign aid is about as helpful as donating a case of lipstick to Sephora. Nor are the isolationist voices on both sides of the aisle helping matters. After all, conservatives aren't alone in mistakenly deprioritizing foreign aid and trade, as we'll see shortly. And it's *easy* to make conservatives look like Scrooges who don't have an ounce of charity in their cold hearts—they're not helping when they don't effectively communicate the reasons why their refusal of aid in some cases is actually because they've found an even more effective way to give aid through another program or policy. That absence of effective public messaging also leaves a vacuum that isolationists and protectionists can step into, gathering political support. This very thing happened during the Clinton presidency.

While President Clinton initially supported regional trade and spearheaded a large number of free trade agreements, he did little to bolster trade in or with Latin America, and his inaction contributed to doldrums of the Latin American economy in the early 2000s. Perhaps President Clinton's trade failures could be traced to procrastination—the last extension of the bill authorizing the White House to "fast track" trade agreements had expired in 1994, yet Clinton waited three years to renew fast track authority, by which time trade relationships with Latin America were already strained.[16] Fast track authority allows the president to force a Congressional vote on any potential trade agreement within 90 days, with no amendments, which makes trade negotiations with America much more appealing to foreign powers, because it prevents regional interests from muddling carefully crafted agreements. Without fast track authority, Clinton had a tough time convincing Latin American countries to play ball, but by the time he did bother to propose reauthorization, a powerful coalition of protectionists on both the right and the left had formed in Congress to oppose it.[17] In fact, his initial support for regional trade deals like the Free Trade Area of the Americas (FTAA) and Asia-Pacific Economic Cooperation (APEC) forum diminished when he failed to secure fast track authority.[18] The *Economist* noted that allowing fast track authority to expire put President Clinton "almost in the dunce's cap."[19]

Without a robust trade agenda, the remainder of the 1990s resulted in missed opportunities for America and an economic and social decline for many Latin America countries. America missed the opportunity to advance its own trade agenda, and to collaborate with Latin America partners on issues ranging from immigration to anti-terrorism to the war on drugs. By the end of the decade, Latin American countries were experiencing economic decline. In fact, the region was poorer in 1998 than it was just ten years earlier.[20] For 2015, the Institute of International Finance expects growth of just 0.2 percent, yet illicit monetary flows out of the region are conservatively estimated at three percent of GDP.[21]

In areas where gender inequality runs rampant, trade can also bring more employment opportunities for women, increasing their autonomy and financial parity with men and even enabling them to get better educations for themselves and their daughters.[22]

Arguably, allowing trade relations with Latin America to flounder could also have had a significant impact on Latin America's female population, who still suffer from systemic wage discrimination.[23]

We all know that poor economic conditions, coupled with weak and corrupt governments, are a magnet for terrorist organizations. Before 9/11, the deadliest terrorist attacks in the Western Hemisphere occurred in Argentina, and in the 1980s, Latin America experienced more terrorist attacks than all other regions combined.[24] The prosecutor assigned to the case for one of these terrorist attacks has since reported the presence of Iranian and Hezbollah cells in several South American countries. And, yet, Latin America has demonstrated a certain irreverence toward global terror. For instance, Brazil does not consider organizations like Hamas or Hezbollah terror groups.[25] Latin America's weak economic performance, informal stance on terror, and proximity to the US mean it should have been, and should continue to be, a priority for America's efforts in good globalization.

Bolstering peace and prosperity via trade is a long cycle. Even when a new trade agreement is put in place, via "fast track" or any other method, it can take years for economies to recover from the loss of trade. And we also can't assume that all nations are simply waiting eagerly to accept whatever trade deal the great America offers them, as soon as protectionism ebbs away from political influence once again. Trade is no different from any deal. Back when I was a venture capitalist, I had the good fortune to encounter renowned angel investor Guy Kawasaki, who taught me that a deal is only a good deal if everyone involved feels like it's a good deal. If one person feels slighted, they'll work hard to unravel the deal, now or in the future. Trade agreements are no different—a good trade agreement has to uphold our American ideals, and what we bring to the table has to be proportional to what's on offer from our trade partners, but there has to be something in it for everyone.

Despite that fact that fifty-two percent of Democratic voters favor free trade, Democratic leaders have really failed on the topic in the recent past. [26] House Speaker Nancy Pelosi amended the House rules to avoid dealing with the Columbia Free Trade Agreement submitted by President Bush in 2008.[27] In its one real trade effort, the Obama administration has negotiated a sweeping trade agreement with Asia, the Trans Pacific Partnership (TPP). However, the administration did so with little-to-no bipartisan engagement, and some purport it would even allow foreign companies to sue America at the federal, state and local level.[28] That is certainly not what we mean when we say an agreement has to have something for everyone!

The problem is that a lack of focus on smart trade agreements creates too many imbalances in the open market. In many cases, these imbalances hurt US businesses and/or pose more risks than a good trade agreement would. The government has made little progress in stemming China's burgeoning intellectual property violations. China essentially steals the idea, or in some cases even the formula or specifications for products, usually because at least a portion of those goods are being made or assembled there, giving the Chinese access to them. China then brands them under a different name and floods the consumer market with these goods at a lower price. This can be deadly for US businesses. Imagine your favorite breakfast protein bar all of a sudden has a competitor that offers what tastes like the same bar but at one dollar cheaper. Pretty soon, the original breakfast bar company is going to be out of business. And while your wallet might be smarting, it may very well be the case that the factory in which that cheaper bar is produced doesn't meet the standards to which the other bar is made.

Intellectual property rights are also an important issue for many female entrepreneurs, who already face inequality in terms of the number of patents and copyrights they hold versus their male counterparts.[29] Enabling women to protect their intellectual property rights can enable women in emerging economies to not only bolster their nation's economic strength, but also forge a more equal path for all women within that nation. For example, female entrepreneur Bethlehem Tilahun Alemu was able to bring prosperity and jobs to her Ethiopian village with her shoe company soleRebels, in part because of the intellectual property protections that allowed her to effectively monetize the designs and techniques that she created.[30] In addition to hurting our wallets or those of individual business leaders, a weak stance on intellectual property protection can harm entire global communities—and even the forward progress of women's rights and economic equality within those communities. Women are a driving force of development in economically struggling countries, but despite many challenges they are emerging as leaders of growth and development, such as in Turkey, which boasts triple the percentage of women running their largest companies, compared to the US.[31] Policies that hinder trade and globalization, or allow intellectual piracy to flourish, have a direct impact on the "third billion"—the women in the third world who are poised to transform the global economy.

In addition to a rampant disrespect for intellectual property rights, many countries, including China, still don't enable the free flow of funds. Instead, successful citizens pack suitcases of cash and take them "on a trip" to Hong Kong where they deposit them in banks to be able to access and spend the money outside the country as they choose. History has shown that when the flow of money is restricted, both illicit activity rises and financial market corrections (in some cases even market crashes) occur. But, China is not the only country with which we need to work harder to create a level financial playing field for entrepreneurs and businesses. For example, as unbelievable as it sounds, Sephora and Walmart are not allowed to expand to India due to a local law that forbids foreign companies which sell multiple brands under one roof from opening retail locations in India. That doesn't sound like a good deal for consumers or business owners.

Just like global trade, foreign aid has to operate within the structure of a deal that works for all parties involved. While foreign aid isn't a direct give-and-take the way trade is, America has to keenly observe the non-monetary benefits of any aid we give, using clearly delineated metrics. Those metrics will vary according to the goal of the aid package, but they can include the reduction of the incidence of certain diseases, the reduction of child poverty, increased access to technology, improved women's rights, and a variety of other humanitarian benefits. Just like with a trade deal, we have to ensure that we're "getting" back, proportionally, what we give—even if what we're "getting" is actually a benefit to the country we're aiding, like a lower infant mortality rate or clean water for the world's poorest communities. In other words, even charity should have what financiers call a return on investment. It is not that the government is trying to make money on its charitable donations, or aid, but it is important that money is yielding the intended results because otherwise it would be better donated elsewhere. But all too often, politicians and diplomats can be seduced by the appearance of charity—for example, by giving in to international pressure to contribute more American money to specific campaigns—rather than the results of that charity.

Without accountability, resources are squandered and results are not achieved. In the U.S. alone, the 50 worst charities direct less than four percent of money raised to actual monetary aid. The amount those charities paid solicitors of donations alone could have paid for mammograms for nearly 10 million uninsured women or built 20,000 Habitat for Humanity homes.[32] Poorly considered foreign aid is similar, but on a much larger scale. When we think about the consequences of millions of dollars that had been given by individuals to charities being squandered, it is heartbreaking to consider the consequences to those in need who truly need help, as well as the wasted potential of all those well-meant dollars. Now imagine that kind of waste and fraud on an international scale, with budgets that only national governments could muster.

One example of the great good that can come when America resists international peer pressure and, instead, puts the focus on results, is global HIV/AIDS relief.

The Global Fund is an international financing organization, supported by private and public donations, created in 2002. It is the largest funder of AIDS, tuberculosis and malaria treatment and prevention programs. The Global Fund receives billions of donations from government sponsors, including the United States and other major world powers, such as France, Japan, Germany, the United Kingdom, and Canada.[33] Since its inception, participation in the Global Fund became a major way for these nations to demonstrate their support for HIV/AIDS relief; the problem was, as with many programs, sometimes momentum outstripped relevance.

Historically, the U.S. has contributed to The Global Fund; the standard for government sponsorships of The Global Fund was for countries to put certain percentage of their GDP toward HIV/AIDS relief. But, bucking tradition, President Bush pushed back against requested amount in 2005. Why? President Bush saw an opportunity to make a more significant contribution toward improving global health, beyond the Global Fund. The Global Fund wasn't quite fulfilling its mission in a manner that met American standards when a 2005 GOA report demonstrated that the Global Fund's Secretariat "did not always base its disbursement recommendations on documented results or even adequate information on expenditures."[34] Liberals expressed outrage at the President's actions, in part because of international pressure on America to contribute more—they were more concerned with keeping up appearances than they were with results.

The Global Fund didn't just fall short on results and metrics; the Bush administration also felt that the numbers were off. While the U.S. contributed the same percentage as other sovereign donors, America was putting in so many more actual dollars because our GDP was much bigger than those of the other contributors. President Bush believed this wasn't necessarily the best way to do it, just because everyone else was doing it. Moreover, he understood the gravity and urgency of the HIV/AIDS epidemic, particularly in Africa. Some companies with operations in Africa were hiring two workers for every one job, simply because the death rate of employees succumbing to AIDS was so high. By 2001, German auto company DaimlerChrysler estimated that twenty percent of its South African workforce was infected with HIV,[35] and Coca Cola committed to use its unparalleled marketing and logistics powers to spread information and treatment for the disease.[36] By 2004, more than 20 million people had died from AIDS, another eight thousand were dying every day, and the number of countries with rapidly rising infected populations was quickly expanding.[37]

Throwing good money after bad never works; defying group think, President Bush set out on an ambitious effort to bring an end to the HIV/AIDS epidemic, particularly in Africa, by creating PEPFAR, the President's Plan for AIDS Relief, an American-administered AIDS relief program with an emphasis on accountability. PEPFAR committed to spend 15 million dollars over five years toward fighting HIV/AIDS. All the while, under the Bush administration, the US remained a leading contributor to the Global Fund.

Within a year of enacting the PEPFAR policy, important results were clear. The only comparable programs in terms of success were non-governmental ones, like the Gates Foundation's progress on fighting malaria. Essentially, President Bush said to the foreign aid policy world, "This doesn't make a lot of sense for us, we can do better"—and then actually did it. His administration increased aid to Africa by more than 640 percent and provided more assistance to the continent than any other president.[38]

PEPFAR is critically important in sheer impact, especially the number of women's lives that it saved—in fact, millions of people have been impacted—coupled with its programmatic accountability. As of 2015, PEPFAR is providing anti-viral support and treatment to 9.5 million people, HIV testing to 18.2 million people, and care for 5.5 million orphans and vulnerable children.[39] The program was reauthorized by President Obama in 2008, and continues to operate today. A recent paper on AIDS relief and research vindicated President Bush's original instincts, "that stable or even increasing investments in HIV does not necessarily mean sustainable programs."[40] The same paper upheld PEPFAR as an example of sustainability. It's also an example of a program that liberals and conservatives can come together on. As President Jimmy Carter said, of President Bush, "Mr. President, let me say that I'm filled with admiration for you and deep gratitude for you about the great contributions you've made to the most needy people on Earth."[41]

Despite these successes, conservatives have their own unique foibles when it comes to aid and trade; liberals aren't the only ones who make missteps. We have a long history of humoring protectionism, the belief that our economy is better off if we exclude trade with other nations or impose punitive tariffs on foreign trade to (in theory) encourage investment, jobs, and commercial activity at home. This approach holds less and less relevance in today's interconnected world, yet it still crops up in a lot of rhetoric about "losing jobs overseas." While trade restrictions are a good way to make sure that human rights violations don't give anyone an unfair advantage (for example, by discouraging child labor), there are other instances where the answer to companies sending jobs overseas is not to punish them, but to try to make it more attractive for them to keep those jobs here or to create new domestic jobs.

The fact is that when companies find effective ways to cut costs, they generally invest those savings in new, higher wage jobs at home, and better products and services for customers. Between 1991 and 2001, U.S.-based multinationals created close to three million jobs overseas. But they also created more than five million jobs domestically. That is significantly higher domestic job creation than that of domestic companies. More recently, that trend has been reversing, but that is not due to the fact that American businesses are seeking cheaper labor or not being patriotic; rather, it is primarily due to a flawed corporate tax structure that has been perpetuated by the Obama administration over the past seven years. Ultimately, corporations focus on growth. The best ones find and use efficiencies to create new jobs that create better products and services. When a job is moved overseas, it does not mean there is ultimately a net job loss here.[42] And, it's worth repeating, those jobs that move overseas—and the trade that flows with them—are helping to lift millions of women out of poverty, expanding the job market so that more women can achieve financial autonomy, and creating more opportunities for women to participate in training and education.[43] All this, and we can still have flourishing economy activity here at home—sounds like a win/win.

Tariffs and restricted trade aren't the only ways that liberals and misled conservatives try to pursue protectionism. For example, some conservatives have, at times, wanted us to call China out on manipulating their currency. These conservatives claim that China manipulates the value of their currency to skew the balance of trade in China's own interests, with a far-reaching effect on American jobs and prosperity. Yet, examining and reporting on China's exchange rate is a Treasury Department task; the Treasury reports on this very issue quarterly to Congress. Nothing's going on that we aren't already meticulously observing; China simply is doing what every other nation with a central bank does.[44] Furthermore, because so many products are made elsewhere but assembled in China (and still bear the "made in China" label), there are many economists who think the accusation of a significantly manipulated currency is mistaken, and that the yuan would not rise nearly as much as accusers expect should China adopt a truly flexible exchange rate. Indeed, in August of 2015, China devalued its currency, saying it would let its currency float--what happens next remains to be seen.[45] But as China's monetary situation unfolds, the U.S. should not get caught up in reactionary rhetoric; instead, the Department of Treasury needs to continue to work with China on free market reforms and on trade policy that have a real, meaningful benefit to the U.S., its workers, and its businesses. While this work should include exchange rate flexibility, to accuse China of manipulation is less impactful than it might appear. Instead of trying to slam China for currency manipulation, we need to focus on setting a level playing field by enhancing American skills and potential.

We may not want to admit it, but in a global economy each nation has to remain competitive, and America is no exception. In

order to succeed, we simply have to be the best. American exceptionalism isn't just about our standing in the world; it is also about
our believing in ourselves. Limiting trade with other countries as
a way to boost our own economy is a disastrous and ineffective
shortcut. We as Americans are lucky to be in situation where we
can win the game. Nothing is easy, but we have many advantages—
freedom, free enterprise, a culture that values success and hard
work, a diverse array of natural resources, and much more.

One of the dangers of globalization is that everyone wants
more. As Americans we shouldn't lose sight of our core values. The
process of a rich life with meaning and purpose will yield more
success and happiness than a focus on having a lot materially at
the endpoint.

Once again, personal accountability is key to our future and
well-being: America is not entitled to success—it was ours to build
and now it's ours to maintain and advance. The attitude that "just
because we had it, it's ours" is a bad example for our children, and
bad for conservatism, and bad for innovation and prosperity. It
will take the hard work and perseverance of each and every one of
us, along with the right policies, to keep America great.

Growing the Pie

Human rights, global development, and capitalism are all intertwined and work together to create a safer and more prosperous
world. Foreign aid is an important part of leadership, diplomacy
and international relations, but as we know, America can't afford
to be a pushover, either. Foreign aid must be strategic—helping
our allies because they help us—and must drive results, so we
can maintain those relationships and keep building a safer, more

prosperous world. Conservatives understand that smart foreign aid leads to good globalization.

Along the same lines, foreign trade is imperative to strong foreign relations and business growth here at home. Trade creates more robust markets around the world, which means more customers for American businesses, a focus on innovation, and enhanced productivity. A good deal is a deal in which everyone believes she wins. Good terms for those overseas, and even outsourcing, can mean those savings result in the reinvestment at home into better jobs, more consumption, and greater financial security. President Clinton abandoned trade with regions like Latin America, and what happened was economic demise, which leads to regional contagion. Now, America is left to pick up the pieces, requiring resources to bail out failing nations and plugging security risks as groups like ISIL seek recruits from depressed areas. So how do we do it *right*?

Foreign aid doesn't work on a cause-of-the-week basis. America must have a clear aid and trade strategy as part of its foreign and economic policies, supported by a clear action plan. We must be consistent in our aid to important allies, such as Israel, while expecting "good behavior" from other nations lining up for American cash and services. The pressure to participate in "cause of the week" giving affects private individuals, public figures, and nations in pretty similar ways. Miss Manners answered a question about "cause of the week" giving just last year, from a letter writer who was boggled by the number of situations in which performers, waiters, and stores urged her to contribute to causes that "aren't necessarily on her philanthropic list."[46] Miss Manners reassured her that she was perfectly within her rights to politely decline, making an aside about how this "cause of the week" panhandling seems to be more and more pervasive, even cropping up at weddings. On a national and international scale, governments can face similar pressure from high-visibility personalities (such as celebrities), other nations, and major non-profits to devote funds to the latest trending charitable cause. But this kind of rudderless aid distribution doesn't help anybody. In aid and trade, good actors should be rewarded. Bad actors, like Russia and China, should not.

When America commits to an aid program, it should be a long-term, sustainable, results-oriented program with a clear tie-in to American interests and/or universal humanitarian concern. If we don't pursue such a strategy, we risk enabling havens for terror; we also miss the opportunity to prevent weak economic markets, fix uneven playing fields, and reverse the heart-wrenching poverty that spills over our borders and affects all of us. As much as we might want to, we don't have the unlimited resources, be it time or capital, to solve all of our own problems, along with those of the world. America can do more and do it better if we are smart about aid and trade.

Diplomacy is another critical component of any aid and trade strategy. We can't exactly trade only with ourselves and we can't stand alone all the time. Our aid and trade strategy needs to be comprised of agreements at both the multilateral and bilateral level. It can be hard to work in a group. Some experts argue the purpose and relevance of some of today's multilateral institutions, like the United Nations (UN), are obsolete. While this argument has some merit, there's value in being part of consensus-driven organizations. We live in a global world and the exchange of ideas and values is imperative to success, even among governments. Sometimes, more minds are better than one.

We also need diplomacy to build support for aid programs. As a White House official, I travelled to South Africa. During meetings with South African leaders, they would gush about former

President Bill Clinton. If I then asked them something in defense of President Bush's work and legacy, like, "What about PEPFAR?" they would say something to the effect of: "PEPFAR saved our country. It's the most important policy enacted by another country for Africa. But Clinton came, he hugged us, he took pictures with us, he kissed our babies." President Bush was more attuned to policy prescriptions, but President Clinton was more warm and fuzzy. Perception is reality, and it's important to maintain the perception that we're all working together because we care. Citizens of the world are no different than US citizens voting—they want to like the candidate as much as they like the policy prescriptions. A brilliant aid package, no matter how well-designed, will not live up to its full potential of advancing American interests if it isn't also accompanied by the diplomacy and public relations required to communicate its worth, and America's goodwill, to people at home and abroad. In that sense, they're similar to trade agreements—they have to be a good deal for both parties, even if the biggest thing America is getting out of it is goodwill.

For real impact, aid and trade must also have measureable results. PEPFAR is a great example of the establishment of a metrics-based aid program. PEPFAR was the largest contribution by any nation to combat a single disease, but it also had to meet Congressionally-mandated targets of effectiveness.[47] PEPFAR alone has averted an estimated 1.2 million deaths, in part because of PEPFAR's unique focus on meeting service delivery goals.[48] Not only do those targets keep us in line, they also help hold our partner countries accountable for meeting goals for delivering services, investing in treatment infrastructure, and spreading training and education about AIDS relief and prevention.[49]

The non-profit sector provides some excellent examples of results-driven aid, and aid with an emphasis on helping other communities help themselves. The Bill and Melinda Gates Foundation's efforts to eradicate malaria worldwide are a great example of goal-driven aid accomplishing outstanding results. Another exemplar non-profit, Technoserve, provides technical support to communities in poverty, instead of dumping money. Technoserve is dedicated to providing resources to small businesses around the world, and the growth of these businesses is amazing. They operate on the "teach a man to fish" principle. This highlights another important principle of foreign aid: that aid has to help other nations get on their feet, not foster dependence on handouts. This was also a foundational principle of PEPFAR, which is also committed to helping the communities it supports build the physical, administrative, and skills infrastructures to take on AIDS treatment and prevention on a local level.

Another effective way to give aid to countries is called "aid for trade." In other words, we aid countries by providing technical resources and, in some cases, financial aid, to develop the infrastructure and processes necessary to engage in trade with other countries. Trade is not just about one country agreeing to exchange goods with another. Countries engaged in trade have to have infrastructure, like ports and roads to move goods, they have to have laws and a system of governing those laws to resolve disputes that may arise, and they have to have safe ways to transport and store money, all things we take for granted in America.[50] These functions constitute what we call "trade capacity," and "aid for trade" is the process of helping other nations build their trade capacity. Enhancing trade capacity is the only way to ensure that global trade (and the benefits that arise from it) is ultimately sustainable. And, by ensuring that the benefits of trade agreements are sustainable, enhancing trade capacity is also an important way to ensure that trade deals are a good deal for all parties involved.

For instance, at Startiste, my startup, we imported beads from India that we had designed to work as component parts that our customer could assemble into their dream product. When our shipment didn't arrive on time, I reached out to my partner in India. "Cathy," he said. "I am so sorry but we've had a monsoon. The roads are closed. Maybe we can send it in a month." The problem was that our store opening was three weeks away at the time. Conditions on the ground, and a country's ability to deal with them, impact that country's business endeavors and thus the livelihood of its citizens. Fortunately, our savvy partner found a way to get us the beads in time, but the episode was an up-close and personal glimpse into the vital importance of building trade capacity in global trading partners.

Sowing the seeds for a country to be a good trading partner requires enormous efforts on the part of the country and its trade partners. I was fortunate to work with truly excellent experts as the United States Trade Representative's Office, the Department of Treasury, and other agencies that spent countless hours helping countries around the world develop the resources to conduct better trade. It's important work: OECD research found that one dollar extra invested in aid for trade generates nearly eight additional dollars of exports from all developing countries—and twenty dollars for the poorest countries.[51]

Aid and trade demonstrate the importance of free markets to developing countries. Rule of law, security of citizens and infrastructure, and the free movement of money are all important components in helping developing countries improve the lives of their citizens and sustain economic growth.

There are also critical but unexpected forms of building trade capacity that have a substantial impact on women's lives around the world. The IMF recommends measures that promote affordable childcare, better access to clean water and sanitation, and access to credit as ways to both bolster economic growth *and* close the gender gap in impoverished nations. In other words, building trade capacity can also result in greater equality for women, lower the female mortality rate, and ensure better education for girls.[52]

And there's a lot of work we can do at home to bolster our own trade environment. The federal government and private sector should work much more closely together. Unfortunately, these two worlds speak different languages despite fairly common goals. Throw on a heaping dose of regulatory burdens from Democrats and there's far less information exchange than there should be. I was shocked that during my time in the White House, only one corporate CEO came in to talk with us about international economic policy. At the presidential level there are certainly interactions and commissions to study issues, but there's not a lot of idea sharing at a more concrete level. While the White House must carefully avoid being lobbied, or the appearance of being lobbied, too heavily by private businesses, it *should* be informed; however, I found it amazing that other corporate leaders didn't seek our team out for a dialogue about how policy affects their businesses, believing the task ended with throwing some cash at a K Street lobbying firm. The private sector should spend a little less time on the transaction of money with lobbyists and a little more time on the transaction of ideas with policymakers to help narrow the stark disconnect between Washington and the corporate sector.

It requires the marshaling of a lot of resources on behalf of America to engage in smart aid and trade, but the results can be astounding. Aid and trade can lead to a reduction of environmental destruction, an increase in democratically elected leaders, improved health and life expectancies, income increases, innovation, and so much more.[53] Give a country a fish, and they'll have fish for a day, but teach a country to fish, and one day they may be selling fish to you!

Value Seven: Paying It Forward

Sometimes the best way to help is to show someone how to help herself. From teaching our kids how to ride their bikes to watching our friends' relationships ups and downs, the road to happiness and prosperity balance the efforts of the village and the willingness of the villager to learn. We must also have a high moral standard; we also know that doing business with a person who doesn't have our best interests at heart, or who is going to use their income to hurt others, isn't good for anyone. These kinds of moral judgments play out on a larger scale in the world in foreign aid and trade.

Contrary to what some protectionist conservatives believe, paying it forward is a fundamentally conservative value. That's because paying it forward is about more than just making ourselves feel better with a token gesture of philanthropy; it's about looking for real results, paying attention to what others need from us, and giving help in a way that lifts *everyone* up. Prosperity, as we've discovered so many times before in this book, is not a zero-sum game. With the right combination of aid and trade, prosperity can be shared, and grown, globally.

Paying it forward isn't an add-on to our existing conservative values; it is their heart. In my own awakening, I realized that it was the string that tied everything else together. Many of the other values described in this book can easily be boiled down to the value of an individual's hard work in building that individual's prosperity. But I knew, all along that, deep down, conservatism isn't just about everyone for herself. This idea of paying it forward is the thing that connects our respect for individual effort and achievement with our desire to make a better world. It's a form of charity and generosity that not only seeks good results—increased prosperity and safety for everyone—but seeks good results through the creation of a good environment—a sustainable global economy that rewards hard work, respect for equality and human rights, and innovation. When we pay it forward, as conservatives, we aren't just offering monetary aid or a few new roads; we're offering, to the rest of the world, the values that made us strong and prosperous.

The right strategy must be at the heart of this outreach, however. Like diplomacy, we have to understand the motives of our partners and their goals as well as our own, and we have to have clear strategy and execute it. We should help our friends, and help them in ways that allow them to help themselves, abetted by metrics of success and a strong emphasis on return on investment. Foreign aid can be a lot like the "donate a suit for job interviews" drive at the church down the street—helping others help themselves. And that ties us back to the beginning: dispelling the belief that conservatives' love of personal responsibility and financial accountability just puts us in a dog-eat-dog world of competition and solitary striving. Actually, conservatives strive for a world very different from that: a world in which everybody helps each other help themselves, so that those who receive help can one day experience the freedom and joy of being independent, prosperous, and free.

Epilogue

My journey to my conservative values was more than political. It was a personal awakening that reverberated through my entire life. It was about more than me; I realized, when I found my own political voice, that I had something to share from my conservative stance that could transform women's lives everywhere.

The years of study and hard work I had committed to advancing my career in business leadership had seemed like the embodiment of everything my family had taught me to value: hard work and building my success from the ground up. It was also the farthest horizon of my conservative beliefs, as much as I was conscious of them at the time: that hard work led to success and satisfaction.

The honor of serving in the White House, as well as my other experiences on Wall Street and Main Street, enabled me to have a very unique perspective on how the sausage of public policy is made, *and* how it tastes when we eat it. In other words, I understood firsthand what policy makers were struggling with, dreaming of, and trying to do in government. But I also knew what it was like to live with those policies personally and professionally as a citizen, entrepreneur, and mother. I was in a unique place to understand the power these policies could bring to women if we brought the same values that guide our personal lives to our policy positions.

I realized that conservatism isn't just a simple equation of "hard work equals success plus satisfaction." It is also about doing good for others, making a difference, serving your family, your friends, your nation, and the world. Conservatism doesn't just have a brain; it has a heart as well.

The culmination of my experiences transformed me in more ways than one. It didn't just revolutionize my politics; it changed my entire outlook on life, on how I viewed being a wife and mother, friend and daughter, mentor and employee. Throughout my life, I've been honored and lucky to learn from truly wise, kind, and incredible men and women, both in government and the private sector. I learned that to truly give of myself to my community, my family, my country, and the world, requires a core set of values that could serve as my anchor through tough times and good times, that can apply to virtually any relationship, that can cut through distinctions of liberal and conservative and define who I was in a way that transcends politics.

My reentry into the corporate world coincided with the phase of my life when I knew I'd soon be trying to start a family—and I knew that wouldn't be an easy road in any respect. As the challenges at work and at home multiplied, I found strength in the notion of service. I felt driven to use my voice to share what I had learned—not just because it would be good for me and my career, but because it would help those around me, starting with my own family. I wanted my girls to grow up seeing me use my voice, so that they'd learn to use their voices too.

Contrary to the misperception of conservatism as a greed-driven ideology, I had discovered that my conservative values fueled me to be more generous. And that same sense of service drove me to write this book, because I deeply believe that sharing these seven values with other women can help us all be the best that we can be, and lift the world up with us.

For too long, conservatives have at times failed to communicate effectively with women, while liberals have managed to win them over on what many perceive to be "women's issues." Liberalism has a longstanding friendship with women as a major force in the women's rights struggle of previous decades, but it's time to take a look in the proverbial mirror, and take a look at our favorite women; they are likely living by many or all of the conservative values laid out in this book. What has long been seen as an oxymoron—the idea of being a strong conservative woman—might be not only possible, but our best self, in reality.

Every issue is a "woman's issue." That's why this book doesn't hold back on any of them, from abortion to foreign policy. We women are multi-faceted; our concerns range further than one small group of policies that directly affect our bodies. Women must be part of the conversation on everything, because we *are* everything. We are mothers, daughters, wives, friends, breadwinners, lawyers, doctors, farmers, teachers, scientists, thinkers, dreamers, the glue that holds society together.

In order to secure the policies that serve us best, we also need the participation of stakeholders, such as business leaders in the private sector, who need to help us ensure that the laws levied upon them work not only for their business models, but also importantly for their customers—us. My experiences in government, Wall Street, and Main Street opened my eyes to the wide disconnect that can exist between these three worlds, and the perceived disconnect between those worlds and our personal, private life. In order to pursue the policies that create a better world for women, we need to embrace the interconnectedness of business, finance, government, security, and global welfare with our own private lives.

Fortunately, connectedness is something women understand innately and deeply. I believe that it's part of our power, and the thing that enables us to succeed, whether we're one of the growing crowds of women becoming doctors or the next female CEO of a Fortune 500 company. In a historic reversal, a recent Pew study finds that young women actually place a higher value on their career success than their male counterparts.[1] That ambition is borne out in the increasing numbers of female enrollments in medical school, law school, and other markers of academic success. Women are now enrolling, and graduating, from college at higher rates than men.[2] This increased focus on success in the outside world seemingly hasn't come at the expense of valuing personal life; women still report valuing family highly, as well.[3] Perhaps that's because we really do understand, innately, how it's all connected.

The thing that translates that interconnectedness into results is the set of values a person lives by. That's why the seven values I've laid out here are so vitally important for all women. By embracing the values of personal responsibility, financial independence, investment in opportunity, belief in the future, strength, and paying it forward, we can convert our interconnectedness into action. We already exercise these values in our daily lives. Women all over the world are discovering their power and coming together to better their own lives and the lives of women around the world by living out these principles. These principles can also help us close the gap between public policy and our private lives, by giving us a framework that applies just as much to political life as it does to personal life. As we work to build a government that embodies these values, we can also inspire and empower the next generation of women, as well.

Who would have thought that, just a few months into my effort to share this story, I would be sitting in the green room of a TV news studio and a lovely woman would ask what kind of work I did. When I told her I was working on a book about women and policy, her face lit up and she urged me to tell her more. A few weeks later, she became my literary agent. It's just one woman's story of bringing her voice to a bigger audience, but it could happen to any of us. I hope you share your experiences with me. I want to continue the conversation about women and policy, because together we are stronger, wiser, and even more powerful.

About the Author

Cathy Lynn Taylor is the translator of policy rhetoric into terms that all American women can understand. An entrepreneur, commentator, and writer, Cathy Lynn makes weekly media appearances on Fox News and other major national media outlets and she blogs at CathyLynnTaylor.com.

With first-hand leadership experience from the White House to Wall Street to Main Street, Cathy Lynn is an expert strategist who is as deeply knowledgeable about national politics as she is about domestic and international policy issues and trends.

Cathy Lynn is a former advisor to President George W. Bush and National Security Council Director for International Finance Policy, a Wall Street business executive, and a Main Street entrepreneur, who has advised the Boards of Silicon Valley start-ups.

Cathy Lynn earned a B.A. in political science from Duke University and her M.B.A. from the Wharton School of the University of Pennsylvania. Her achievements have been recognized by the media, including the *Wall Street Journal*, ABC News, and the *New York Post*. She served an appointment by President Bush as a White House Fellow and is a member of the Council on Foreign Relations.

A former model, wife, and mother of two young daughters, Cathy Lynn is an avid champion and opinion leader of women's issues. She resides near New York City with her husband and two young daughters.

Endnotes

PREFACE

1 Gillian B. White, "Women Are Owning More and More Small Businesses," *The Atlantic*, April 17, 2015, http://www.theatlantic.com/business/archive/2015/04/women-are-owning-more-and-more-small-businesses/390642/
2 https://www.aamc.org/download/321442/data/factstable1.pdf
3 "A Current Glance at Women in the Law," The American Bar Association—Commission on Women in the Profession, July 2014, http://www.americanbar.org/content/dam/aba/marketing/women/current_glance_statistics_july2014.authcheckdam.pdf
4 Wendy Wang, Kim Parker, and Paul Taylor, "Breadwinner Moms," *Pew Research* Center, May 29, 2013, http://www.pewsocialtrends.org/2013/05/29/breadwinner-moms/
5 Frank Newport, "Women More Likely to Be Democrats, Regardless of Age," Gallup, June 12, 2009, http://www.gallup.com/poll/120839/women-likely-democrats-regardless-age.aspx
6 "Women in State Legislatures: 2011 Legislative Session," National Conference of State Legislatures, November 21, 2011, http://www.ncsl.org/legislators-staff/legislators/womens-legislative-network/women-in-state-legislatures-2011.aspx

CHAPTER 1

1 "If You Are Not a Liberal at 25 You Have No Heart. If You Are Not a Conservative at 35 You Have No Brain," Quote Investigator, February 24, 2014, http://quoteinvestigator.com/2014/02/24/heart-head/
2 Meredith Clark, "6 Anti-woman policies Scott Walker may want voters to forget," MSNBC.com, October 9, 2014, http://www.msnbc.com/msnbc/6-anti-woman-policies-scott-walker
3 Louis Jacobson, "In Context: Does Mitt Romney like firing people?," *Politifact*, January 11, 2012, http://www.politifact.com/truth-o-meter/article/2012/jan/11/context-does-mitt-romney-firing-people/
4 https://www.pyschologytoday.com/blog/the-power-prime/201002/parenting-the-sad-misuse-self-esteem
5 Leslie Lenkowsky, "Big Philanthropy," *The Wilson Quarterly*, Winter 2007, http://archive.wilsonquarterly.com/essays/big-philanthropy

6 Barbara J. Elliott, "Remembering Reagan's Compassion," *The Imaginative Conservative*, September 18, 2010, http://www.theimaginativeconservative.org /2010/09/remembering-reagan-compassion.html

7 Leslie Lenkowsky, "Ronald Reagan Helped Philanthropy, Despite How Much Nonprofit World Objected to his Policies," *The Chronicle of Philanthropy*, June 10, 2004, https://philanthropy.com/article/Ronald-Reagan-Helped/168649

8 John Grgurich, "Who's More Generous, Liberals or Conservatives?," *The Fiscal Times*, October 17, 2014, http://www.thefiscaltimes.com/2014/10/17 /Who-s-More-Generous-Liberals-or-Conservatives

9 Peter Edelman, "The Worst Thing Bill Clinton Has Done," *The Atlantic*, March 1997, http://www.theatlantic.com/magazine/archive/1997/03/the-worst-thing -bill-clinton-has-done/376797/

10 Richard Morin and Claudia Deane, "Sole Searching for a Heritage Scholar," *The Washington Post*, March 19, 2002, https://www.washingtonpost.com /archive/politics/2002/03/19/sole-searching-for-a-heritage-scholar /aab7fdca-0ec9-478f-a150-8f4a5feda988/

11 Bryce Covert, "Clinton Touts Welfare Reform. Here's How It Failed," *The Nation*, September 6, 2012, http://www.thenation.com/article/clinton-touts -welfare-reform-heres-how-it-failed/

12 Bryce Covert, "Clinton Touts Welfare Reform. Here's How It Failed," *The Nation*, September 6, 2012, http://www.thenation.com/article/clinton-touts -welfare-reform-heres-how-it-failed/, emphasis added

13 Liz Schott, Ladonna Pavetti, and Ife Finch, "How States Have Spent Federal and State Funds Under the TANF Block Grant," Center on Budget and Policy Priorities, August 8, 2012, http://www.cbpp.org/research/how-states -have-spent-federal-and-state-funds-under-the-tanf-block-grant?fa =view&id=3808

14 Steve Straub, "The Top 5 Ways Liberal Policies Hurt the Poor," The Federalist Papers Project, accessed on March 16, 2016, http://www.thefederalistpapers. org/us/the-top-5-ways-liberal-policies-hurt-the-poor

15 Molly Moorhead, "Romney Campaign says women were hit hard by job losses under Obama," *Politifact*, April 10, 2012, http://www.politifact.com /truth-o-meter/statements/2012/apr/10/mitt-romney/romney-campaign -says-women-were-hit-hard-job-losse/

16 Greg Richter, "Fiorina: Fact-Checkers Were Right on Women's Jobs, but Liberal Policies Still Bad," *NewsMax*, November 1, 2015, http://www.newsmax.com /Politics/carly-fiorina-wrong-statements-women/2015/11/01/id/700014/

17 Zachary A. Goldfarb, "Male-female pay gap remains entrenched at White House," *The Washington Post*, July 1, 2014, https://www.washingtonpost.com /politics/malefmale-pay-gap-remains-entrenched-at-white-house/2014 /07/01/dbc6c088-0155-11e4-8fd0-3a663dfa68ac_story.html

18 Stephen Moore, "The liberal war on women," *The Washington Times*, October 25, 2015, http://www.washingtontimes.com/news/2015/oct/25/stephen-moore -the-liberal-war-on-women/

19 Ibid.

20 Ibid.

21 "21.3 Percent of U.S. Population Participates in Government Assistance Programs Each Month," United States Census Bureau, May 28, 2015, https:// www.census.gov/newsroom/press-releases/2015/cb15-97.html

22 To learn more about The New Deal, check out the Further Reading section at the end of this book

23 Robert Rector, "The Redistributive State: The Allocation of Government Benefits, Services, and Taxes in the United States," The Heritage Founda-tion, September 15, 2015, http://www.heritage.org/research/reports/2015/09 /the-redistributive-state-the-allocation-of-government-benefits-services -and-taxes-in-the-united-states

24 Robert Rector, "Married to the welfare state," The Heritage Foundation, February 10, 2015, http://www.heritage.org/research/commentary/2015/2 /married-to-the-welfare-state

25 Stephen Dinan, "Welfare spending jumps 32% during Obama's presidency," *The Washington Times*, October 18, 2012, http://www.washingtontimes.com /news/2012/oct/18/welfare-spending-jumps-32-percent-four-years/?page=all

26 "Improper Payments: Government-Wide Estimates and Use of Death Data to Help Prevent Payments to Deceased Individuals," U.S. Government Account-ability Office, March 16, 2015, GOA-15-482T, http://www.gao.gov/products /GAO-15-482T

27 Amy Sherman, "Scott abandons promise to drug test welfare recipients," *Politi-fact Florida,* March 10, 2015, http://www.politifact.com/florida/promises /scott-o-meter/promise/600/require-drug-screening-for-welfare-recipients/

28 Ibid.

29 "Directory of Federally Funded Prevention Programs," accessed March 16, 2016, https://www.whitehouse.gov/ondcp/federally-funded-prevention -programs

30 "Block Grants for Prevention and Treatment of Substance Abuse," accessed March 16, 2016, https://www.whitehouse.gov/sites/default/files/ondcp /prevention/block_grants_for_prevention_and_treatment_of_substance _abuse.pdf

31 "Labor Market Effects of the Affordable Care Act: Updated Estimates," Congressional Budget Office, February 2014, https://www.cbo.gov/sites /default/files/cbofiles/attachments/45010-breakout-AppendixC.pdf

32 Ibid.

33 Jeff Sessions, "The 'Welfare Cliff': How The Benefit Scale Discourages Work," United States Senate Budget Committee, accessed March 16, 2016, http://www.budget.senate.gov/republican/public/index.cfm/files/serve/?File_id =b5c0680b-d78d-4e00-b4f7-00b5d2a8816a

34 Ibid.

35 Nicholas Kristof, "Profiting From a Child's Illiteracy," *The New York Times,* December 7, 2012, http://www.nytimes.com/2012/12/09/opinion/sunday/ kristof-profiting-from-a-childs-illiteracy.html?pagewanted=all

36 Abort73.com, "Worldwide Abortion Statistics," Loxafamosity Ministries, last updated May 26, 2011, http://www.abort73.com/abortion_facts/worldwide _abortion_statistics/

37 Ibid.

38 "State Legislative Center," National Right to Life, accessed March 16, 2016, http://www.nrlc.org/statelegislation/

39 All preceding stats from this paragraph are from: Sandra Yin, "Abortion in the United States and the World," Population Reference Bureau, December 2005, http://www.prb.org/Publications/Articles/2005/AbortionintheUnited StatesandtheWorld.aspx

40 Robert Rector, "How Welfare Undermines Marriage and What to Do About It," The Heritage Foundation, November 17, 2014, http://www.heritage.org/ research/reports/2014/11/how-welfare-undermines-marriage-and-what -to-do-about-it

41 "America's Changing Religious Landscape," Pew Research Center, May 12, 2015, http://www.pewforum.org/2015/05/12/americas-changing-religious -landscape/

42 Thomas Jefferson, *To George Wythe Paris, August 13, 1786,* Letter. From American History From the Revolution to Reconstruction and beyond, accessed March 16, 2016, http://www.let.rug.nl/usa/presidents/thomas -jefferson/letters-of-thomas-jefferson/jefl47.php

43 Jon Queally, "'A Nation in Decline': Majority of US Public School Students Live in Poverty," Common Dreams, January 17, 2015, http://www.commondreams .org/news/2015/01/17/nation-decline-majority-us-public-school-students -live-poverty

44 James Marshall Crotty, "7 Signs That U.S. Education Decline Is Jeopardiz-ing Its National Security," *Forbes,* March 26, 2012, http://www.forbes.com /sites/jamesmarshallcrotty/2012/03/26/7-signs-that-americas-educational -decline-is-jeopardizing-its-national-security/

45 "Every Student Succeeds Act," U.S. Department of Education, accessed on March 16, 2016, http://www.ed.gov/esea

46 Jeanne Allen, "Conservative Education Reform That Conservatives Misun-derstand," *National Review*, April 7, 2015, http://www.nationalreview.com

/article/416528/conservative-education-reform-conservatives-misunderstand
-jeanne-allen

47 Louis V. Gerstner Jr., "Lessons From 40 Years of Education 'Reform,'"
    The Wall Street Journal, December 1, 2008, http://www.wsj.com/articles
    /SB122809533452168067

48 "'Rubber Rooms' In New York Schools Cost City $22 Million A Year For
    Teachers Awaiting Hearings," *The Huffington Post,* October 16, 2012, http://
    www.huffingtonpost.com/2012/10/16/rubber-rooms-in-new-york-city-22
    -million_n_1969749.html

49 "School Choice," Institute for Justice, accessed March 16, 2016, http://ij.org
    /pillar/school-choice/?post_type=case

50 Diana Furchtgott-Roth and Jared Meyer, "Teachers' Unions Throw Students
    Under the Bus," Real Clear Markets, May 7, 2015, http://www.realclearmarkets
    .com/articles/2015/05/07/teachers_unions_throw_students_under_the_bus
    _101655.html

51 "Fast Facts: Dropout rates," National Center for Education Statistics, Institute
    of Education Sciences, accessed March 16, 2016, https://nces.ed.gov/fastfacts
    /display.asp?id=16

52 Julie Hirschfeld Davis, "President Obama Signs Into Law a Rewrite of No
    child Left Behind," *The New York Times,* December 10, 2015, http://www
    .nytimes.com/2015/12/11/us/politics/president-obama-signs-into-law-a
    -rewrite-of-no-child-left-behind.html?_r=0

53 Rachel Curtis, "Finding a New Way: Leveraging Teacher Leadership to Meet
    Unprecedented Demands," The Aspen Institute, February 2013, http://www.
    aspendrl.org/portal/browse/DocumentDetail?documentId=1574&download

54 Emily Richmond, "America's Teacher-Training Programs Aren't Good Enough,"
    The Atlantic, June 18, 2013, http://www.theatlantic.com/national/archive
    /2013/06/americas-teacher-training-programs-arent-good-enough/276993/

55 Arthur Levine, "Educating School Teachers," The Education Schools Project,
    2006, http://www.edschools.org/pdf/Educating_Teachers_Report.pdf

56 "TFA on the Record," Teach for America, accessed March 16, 2016, https://
    www.teachforamerica.org/tfa-on-the-record

57 Gary Ravani, "Why public education needs teachers unions," EdSource, July 27,
    2014, http://edsource.org/2014/why-public-education-needs-teachers-unions
    /65723

58 Sally Lovejoy and Chad Miller, "Collective Bargaining and Student Academic
    Achievement," American Action Forum, June 2013, http://americanaction
    forum.org/uploads/files/research/Collective_Bargaining.pdf

59 Linda Gorman, "School Choice Raises Student Achievement," The National
    Bureau of Economic Research, accessed March 16, 2016, http://www.nber
    .org/digest/aug02/w8873.html

60 Nina Rees and Andrew Broy, "Study: Charter High Schools Have 7–11% Higher Graduation Rates Than Their Public School Peers," *Forbes,* March 17, 2014, http://www.forbes.com/sites/realspin/2014/03/17/study-charter-high-schools-have-7-11-higher-graduation-rates-than-their-public-school-peers/

61 Matthew M. Chingos and Paul E. Peterson, "A Generation of School-Voucher Success," *The Wall Street Journal,* August 23, 2012, http://www.wsj.com/articles/SB10000872396390444184704577585582150808386

62 Dacia Toll, "Fund all Connecticut students fairly and equitably," *The New Hampshire Register,* November 15, 2015, http://www.nhregister.com/opinion/20151115/dacia-toll-fund-all-connecticut-students-fairly-and-equitably

63 http://ies.ed.gov/ncee/pubs/20104018/pdf/20104018.pdf

64 Jeanne Allen, "Conservative Education Reform Conservatives Misunderstand," *National Review,* April 7, 2015, http://www.nationalreview.com/article/416528/conservative-education-reform-conservatives-misunderstand-jeanne-allen

65 Kwame Anthony Appiah, "Should My Rich Friends Apply for Financial Aid?," *The New York Times Magazine,* November 25, 2015, http://www.nytimes.com/2015/11/29/magazine/should-my-rich-friends-apply-for-financial-aid.html

66 Ibid.

CHAPTER 2

1 Gillian B. White, "Women Are Owning More and More Small Businesses," *The Atlantic,* April 17, 2015, http://www.theatlantic.com/business/archive/2015/04/women-are-owning-more-and-more-small-businesses/390642/

2 https://www.aamc.org/download/321442/data/factstable1.pdf

3 "A Current Glance at Women in the Law," The American Bar Association—Commission on Women in the Profession, July 2014, http://www.americanbar.org/content/dam/aba/marketing/women/current_glance_statistics_july2014.authcheckdam.pdf

4 Wendy Wang, Kim Parker, and Paul Taylor, "Breadwinner Moms," *Pew Research* Center, May 29, 2013, http://www.pewsocialtrends.org/2013/05/29/breadwinner-moms/

5 Reem Heakal, "What Is Fiscal Policy?," Investopedia, accessed March 16, 2016, http://www.investopedia.com/articles/04/051904.asp

6 "Historical Tables," Office of Management and Budget, accessed on March 16, 2016, https://www.whitehouse.gov/omb/budget/Historicals

7 Romina Boccia, "Federal Spending by the Numbers, 2014: Government Spending Trends in Graphics, Tables, and Key Points (Including 51 Examples of Government Waste)," The Heritage Foundation, December 8, 2014, http://www.heritage.org/research/reports/2014/12/federal-spending-by-the-numbers-2014

8   "Federal Spending: Where Does the Money Go," National Priorities Project, accessed on March 16, 2016, https://www.nationalpriorities.org/budget-basics /federal-budget-101/spending/

9   Andrew Chung, "The link between appliances and feminism," thestar.com, April 5, 20009, http://www.thestar.com/news/insight/2009/04/05/the_link _between_appliances_and_feminism.html

10 "The Debt to the Penny and Who Holds It," TreasuryDirect.gov, accessed on March 16, 2016, http://treasurydirect.gov/NP/debt/current

11 Crutsinger, Martin, "World Bank Calls on Rich Countries to Forgive Two-thirds of Iraq's Debt," Associated Press, October 29, 2003

12 "Measuring Stability and Security in Iraq," GlobalSecurity.org, June 2007, http://www.globalsecurity.org/military/library/report/2007/iraq-security -stability_jun2007-01-2.htm

13 James D. Agresti, "National Debt Facts," Just Facts, last updated March 2, 2016, http://www.justfacts.com/nationaldebt.asp

14 Ibid.

15 "Policy Basics: Where Do Our Federal Tax Dollars Go?," Center on Budget and Policy Priorities, last updated March 4, 2016, http://www.cbpp.org /research/policy-basics-where-do-our-federal-tax-dollars-go

16 Susan K. Urahn, Travis Plunkett, Erin Currier, Diana Elliott, Sarah Sattelmeyer, and Denise Wilson, "Women's Work: The economic mobility of women across a generation," Pew Charitable Trusts, April 2014, http://www.pewtrusts.org/en/research-and-analysis/reports/2014/04/01 /womens-work-the-economic-mobility-of-women-across-a-generation

17 Catherine Rampell, "U.S. Women on the Rise as Family Breadwinner," *The New York Times*, May 29, 2013, http://www.nytimes.com/2013/05/30/busi-ness/economy/women-as-family-breadwinner-on-the-rise-study-says.html

18 Tina Orem, "Survey: Millennials fear tax season more than other age groups do," *USA Today*, February 19, 2016, http://www.usatoday.com/story/money /personalfinance/2016/02/17/survey-millennials-fear-tax-season-more -than-other-age-groups-do/80315344/

19 Susan K. Urahn, Travis Plunkett, Erin Currier, Diana Elliott, Sarah Sattelmeyer, and Denise Wilson, "Women's Work: The economic mobility of women across a generation," Pew Charitable Trusts, April 2014, http://www.pewtrusts.org/en/research-and-analysis/reports/2014/04/01 /womens-work-the-economic-mobility-of-women-across-a-generation

20 Scott Lilly, "Is Redistributing Wealth a Bad Thing? You Betcha!," Center for American Progress, October 21, 2008, https://www.americanprogress .org/issues/economy/news/2008/10/21/5132/is-redistributing-wealth -a-bad-thing-you-betcha/

21 Jo Craven McGinty, "Middle Class, Undefined: How Purchasing Power Affects Perceptions of Wealth," *The Wall Street Journal,* February 20, 2015, http://www.wsj.com/articles/middle-class-undefined-how-purchasing-power-affects-perceptions-of-wealth-1424449343

22 "The Federal Budget in Pictures," The Heritage Foundation, accessed on March 16, 2016, http://www.heritage.org/federalbudget/top10-percent-income-earners

23 Laura Saunders, "Top 20% of Earners Pay 84% of Income Tax," *The Wall Street Journal,* April 10, 2015, http://www.wsj.com/articles/top-20-of-earners-pay-84-of-income-tax-1428674384

24 Andy Kiersz, "There's A Visible Glass Ceiling For Top Female Earners In These 3 Charts," *Business Insider,* October 27, 2014, http://www.businessinsider.com/gender-glass-ceiling-for-top-earners-2014-10

25 Louis Woodhill, "Rising Wealth Inequality Is Bad, But Liberal 'Solutions' Are Much Worse," *Forbes,* October 9, 2013, http://www.forbes.com/sites/louiswoodhill/2013/10/09/rising-wealth-inequality-is-bad-but-liberal-solutions-are-much-worse/

26 Jeffrey Dorfman, "The Neglected Cost of Government Spending," *Real Clear Markets,* February 11, 2013, http://www.realclearmarkets.com/articles/2013/02/11/the_neglected_cost_of_government_spending_100139.html

27 Walter Williams, "Wealth redistribution is bad solution for income inequality," *Lubbock Avalanche-Journal,* January 20, 2014, http://lubbockonline.com/editorial-columnists/2014-01-20/williams-wealth-redistribution-bad-solution-income-inequality#.VmuWJ9IrKW9

28 Ed Kaplan, "Does Taxing the Wealthy Hurt Growth?," The Economist's View, October 25, 2012, http://economistsview.typepad.com/economistsview/2012/10/does-taxing-the-wealthy-hurt-growth.html

29 Richard Posner, "Does Redistributing Income from Rich to Poor Increase or Reduce Economic Growth or Welfare?," The Becker-Posner Blog, December 29, 2013, http://www.becker-posner-blog.com/2013/12/does-redistributing-income-from-rich-to-poor-increase-or-reduce-economic-growth-or-welfare-posner.html

30 Brian M. Riedl, "Why Government Spending Does Not Stimulate Economic Growth," The Heritage Foundation, November 12, 2008, http://www.heritage.org/research/reports/2008/11/why-government-spending-does-not-stimulate-economic-growth

31 Thomas Stratmann and Gabriel Lucjan Okolski, "Does Government Spending Affect Economic Growth?," The Mercatus Center, June 10, 2010, http://mercatus.org/publication/does-government-spending-affect-economic-growth

32 Shwetlena Sabarwal, Nistha Sinha, and Mayra Buvinic, "How Do Women Weather Economic Shocks? What We Know," The World Bank, January 2011, http://siteresources.worldbank.org/INTPREMNET/Resources/EP46.pdf

33 Sean Pool, "The High Return on Investment for Publicly Funded Research," The Center for American Progress, December 10, 2012, https://www.americanprogress.org/issues/economy/report/2012/12/10/47481/the-high-return-on-investment-for-publicly-funded-research/

34 "Flat Tax," Investopedia.com, accessed on March 17, 2016, http://www.investopedia.com/terms/f/flattax.asp?no_header_alt=true

35 Kelly Phillips Erb, "Our Current Tax v. The Flat Tax v. The Fair Tax: What's The Difference?," Forbes, August 7, 2015, http://www.forbes.com/sites/kellyphillipserb/2015/08/07/our-current-tax-v-the-flat-tax-v-the-fair-tax-whats-the-difference/

36 http://opportunity.heritage.org/cut-spending-fix-the-debt-and-reform-entitlements/

37 "Policy Basics: Where Do Our Federal Tax Dollars Go?," Center on Budget and Policy Priorities, last updated March 4, 2016, http://www.cbpp.org/research/policy-basics-where-do-our-federal-tax-dollars-go

38 Becca Aaronson, "How Privatized Social Security Works in Galveston," The New York Times, September 17, 2011, http://www.nytimes.com/2011/09/18/us/how-privatized-social-security-works-in-galveston.html

39 Barbara E. Kritzer, "Privatizing Social Security: The Chilean Experience," Social Security Bulletin, Social Security Administration, Fall 1996, https://www.ssa.gov/policy/docs/ssb/v59n3/v59n3p45.pdf

40 "2015 Federal Tax Rates, Personal Exemptions, and Standard Deductions," IRS.com, accessed on March 17, 2016, http://www.irs.com/articles/2015-federal-tax-rates-personal-exemptions-and-standard-deductions

CHAPTER 3

1 Matthew Boesler, "WEIMAR: Here's What We Know About The Hyperinflation Horror Story That Haunts Europe Today," Business Insider, October 21, 2012, http://www.businessinsider.com/weimar-the-real-story-of-the-devastating-collapse-that-haunts-the-eurozone-today-2012-10?op=1

2 Karen E. Klein, "Rise of Female Angel Investors Fuels Women-Run Companies," Bloomberg Business, September 11, 2014, http://www.bloomberg.com/bw/articles/2014-09-10/angel-investing-rise-of-women-investors-fuels-women-run-companies

3 Jeff Cox, "Fed Raises Rates by 25 Basis Points, First Since 2006," CNBC.com, December 16, 2015, http://www.cnbc.com/2015/12/16/fed-raises-rates-for-first-time-since-2006.html

4 Michelle Lodge, "Female breadwinners: What it means when mom is the provider," Fortune, November 3, 2014, http://fortune.com/2014/11/03/female-breadwinners/

5   Foley & Lardner LLP, "Foley Study Reveals Continued High Cost of Being Public," Foley.com, August 2, 2007, https://www.foley.com/foley-study-reveals -continued-high-cost-of-being-public-08-02-2007/

6   "Say goodbye to traditional free checking," The Associated Press, October 25, 2010, http://www.syracuse.com/news/index.ssf/2010/10/say_goodbye_to _traditional_fre.html

7   Heather Long, "Female investors often beat men," CNN Money, Feburary 19, 2015, http://money.cnn.com/2015/02/19/investing/investing-women-men/

8   "Monetary Policy," Amosweb.com, accessed on March 18, 2016, http://www .amosweb.com/cgi-bin/awb_nav.pl?s=wpd&c=dsp&k=monetary+policy

9   Steven Plaut, "Does Scandinavian Socialism Work?" *Frontpage Magazine*, August 11, 2011, http://www.frontpagemag.com/fpm/101480/does-scandinavian -socialism-work-steven-plaut

10 "The Scandivavian Socialism Utopia Is Bullshit," Bullshit Exposed, December 6, 2012, http://www.bullshitexposed.com/scandinavian-socialism -debunked/

CHAPTER 4

1   Jie Zong and Jeanne Batalova, "Frequently Requested Statistics on Immigrants and Immigration in the United States," Migration Policy Institute, February 26, 2015, http://www.migrationpolicy.org/article /frequently-requested-statistics-immigrants-and-immigration-united-states

2   Phillip Connor, "5 challenges to estimating global migration," Pew Research Center, October 25, 2013, http://www.pewresearch.org/fact-tank /2013/10/25/5-challenges-to-estimating-global-migration/

3   Jens Manuel Krogstad and Michael Keegan, "From Germany to Mexico: How America's source of immigrants has changed over a century," Pew Research Center, October 7, 2015, http://www.pewresearch.org/fact-tank/2015/10/07/ a-shift-from-germany-to-mexico-for-americas-immigrants/

4   "Milestones: 1921–1936," U.S. Department of State Office of the Historian, accessed March 18, 2016, https://history.state.gov/milestones/1921-1936 /immigration-act

5   "Modern Immigration Wave Brings 59 Million to U.S., Driving Population Growth and Change Through 2065: View of Immigration's Impact on U.S. Society Mixed," Pew Research Center, September 2015.

6   Ibid.

7   "Holocaust Encyclopedia: Refugees," United States Holocaust Memorial Museum, accessed March 18, 2016, http://www.ushmm.org/wlc/en/article .php?ModuleId=10005139

8   "Directory of Visa Categories," Travel.State.Gov, accessed March 18, 2016, https://travel.state.gov/content/visas/en/general/all-visa-categories.html

9   Ariel G. Ruiz, Jie Zong, and Jeanne Batalova, "Immigrant Women in the United States," Migration Policy Institute, March 20, 2015, http://www.migrationpolicy .org/article/immigrant-women-united-states

10 James Dao, "Vietnam Legacy: Finding G.I. Fathers, and Children Left Behind," *The New York Times,* September 15, 2013, http://www.nytimes.com /2013/09/16/us/vietnam-legacy-finding-gi-fathers-and-children-left -behind.html

11 Ibid.

12 Jens Manuel Krogstad and Jeffrey S. Passel, "5 facts about illegal immigration in the U.S.," Pew Research Center, November 19, 2015, http://www.pewresearch .org/fact-tank/2015/11/19/5-facts-about-illegal-immigration-in-the-u-s/

13 Jie Zong and Jeanne Batalova, "Frequently Requested Statistics on Immigrants and Immigration in the United States," Migration Policy Institute, February 26, 2015, http://www.migrationpolicy.org/article /frequently-requested-statistics-immigrants-and-immigration-united-states

14 Jens Manuel Krogstad and Jeffrey S. Passel, "5 facts about illegal immigration in the U.S.," Pew Research Center, November 19, 2015, http://www.pewresearch .org/fact-tank/2015/11/19/5-facts-about-illegal-immigration-in-the-u-s/

15 Jie Zong and Jeanne Batalova, "Frequently Requested Statistics on Immigrants and Immigration in the United States," Migration Policy Institute, February 26, 2015, http://www.migrationpolicy.org/article/frequently-requested -statistics-immigrants-and-immigration-united-states

16 Max Fisher, "A revealing map of who wants to move to the U.S.," *The Washington Post,* March 22, 2013, https://www.washingtonpost.com/news/worldviews /wp/2013/03/22/a-revealing-map-of-who-wants-to-move-to-the-u-s/

17 Ariel G. Ruiz, Jie Zong, and Jeanne Batalova, "Immigrant Women in the United States," Migration Policy Institute, March 20, 2015, http://www.migrationpolicy .org/article/immigrant-women-united-states

18 http://www.renewoureconomy.org/sites/all/themes/pnae/img/new-american -fortune-500-june-2011.pdf

19 http://nvca.org/research/stats-studies/

20 http://www.migrationpolicy.org/article/foreign-born-health-care-workers -united-states

21 https://www.nsf.gov/news/news_summ.jsp?cntn_id=136430&org=NSF &from=news

22 http://reports.weforum.org/global-gender-gap-report-2015/economies /#economy=USA

23 https://www.cbo.gov/sites/default/files/110th-congress-2007-2008/reports /12-6-immigration.pdf

24 http://www.migrationpolicy.org/research/immigrants-and-wioa-ser- vices-comparison-sociodemographic-characteristics-native-and-foreign

25 Ibid.

26 http://www.latimes.com/nation/la-na-san-bernardino-shooters-preplanning -20151209-story.html

27 http://www.nytimes.com/2013/01/08/us/huge-amounts-spent-on -immigration-study-finds.html

28 http://www.wsj.com/articles/the-mythical-connection-between -immigrants-and-crime-1436916798

29 http://www.wsj.com/articles/SB1000142412788732370670457822812055905 7666

30 Jie Zong and Jeanne Batalova, "Frequently Requested Statistics on Immigrants and Immigration in the United States," Migration Policy Institute, February 26, 2015, http://www.migrationpolicy.org/article /frequently-requested-statistics-immigrants-and-immigration-united-states

31 http://www.pewresearch.org/fact-tank/2015/07/24/5-facts-about-illegal -immigration-in-the-u-s/

32 http://www.wsj.com/articles/a-syrian-refugee-lesson-for-liberals -1447719595

33 http://www.cfr.org/religion/europes-angry-muslims/p8218

34 http://www.economist.com/blogs/graphicdetail/2015/11/daily-chart-10

35 http://www.migrationpolicy.org/article/refugees-and-asylees-united-states

36 Ibid.

37 http://www.state.gov/j/prm/ra/

38 Ibid.

39 http://www.pewresearch.org/fact-tank/2015/11/19/u-s-public-seldom-has -welcomed-refugees-into-country/

40 http://www.theguardian.com/us-news/2015/nov/19/syrian-refugees-in -america-fact-from-fiction-congress

41 Ibid.

42 Ibid.

43 http://blogs.findlaw.com/blotter/2014/07/is-illegal-immigration-a-crime -improper-entry-v-unlawful-presence.html

CHAPTER 5

1 https://www.monticello.org/site/jefferson/empire-liberty-quotation

2 https://history.state.gov/milestones/1937-1945/american-isolationism

3 http://www.whitehousemuseum.org/furnishings/resolute-desk.htm

4 http://blogs.reuters.com/great-debate/2015/05/13/just-how-special-is-the -u-s-britain-special-relationship/

5 http://www.telegraph.co.uk/news/politics/11345045/Our-special-relationship -hangs-by-a-thread.html

6 http://www.breitbart.com/video/2012/09/14/flashback-obama-the-day -im-inaugurated-muslim-hostility-will-ease/

7   http://www.nbcnews.com/news/us-news/state-dept-35-increase-terrorist
    -attacks-worldwide-n378416
8   http://www.independent.co.uk/news/world/middle-east/life-as-a-woman
    -under-isis-document-reveals-for-the-first-time-what-group-really-expects
    -from-female-10025143.html
9   http://www.pbs.org/wgbh/americanexperience/features/general-article
    /carter-hostage-crisis/
10 https://criticalpolitics.wordpress.com/2009/04/07/reagan-we-can-have
    -peace-this-second-if-we-surrender/
11 Ibid.
12 http://time.com/2819889/obama-russia-europe-poland/
13 http://freebeacon.com/national-security/clinton-russian-reset-brilliant
    -stroke/
14 http://time.com/2819889/obama-russia-europe-poland/
15 http://humanrightshouse.org/Articles/7821.html
16 http://www.economist.com/news/leaders/21669950-danger-russias
    -intervention-syria-and-americas-timidity-afghanistan-putin-dares
17 http://www.pewglobal.org/2015/06/23/1-americas-global-image/
18 Ibid.
19 Ibid.
20 Ibid.
21 Ibid.
22 http://www.pewglobal.org/2015/06/23/2-views-of-china-and-the-global
    -balance-of-power/
23 Ibid.
24 http://diplomacy.state.gov/discoverdiplomacy/
25 https://www.federalregister.gov/agencies
26 http://www.pewresearch.org/fact-tank/2015/03/12/how-do-americans
    -stand-out-from-the-rest-of-the-world/
27 http://www.gallup.com/poll/153992/150-million-adults-worldwide-migrate
    .aspx
28 http://www.abc.net.au/news/2004-02-01/iraq-awards-foreign-bank
    -licences/128654

CHAPTER 6

1   http://www.cnn.com/2013/01/24/us/military-women-glance/
2   http://archive.defense.gov/home/features/2015/0315_womens-history/
3   http://time.com/4137854/military-women-draft/
4   http://www.military.com/deployment/effects-deployment-families.html
5   Ibid.

6   Center for Strategic and Budgetary Assessments. *Assessment of the FY 2015 Defense Budget*. By Todd Harrison. Washington, DC: Center for Strategic and Budgetary Assessments, 2014.

7   https://history.state.gov/milestones/1945-1952/creation-israel

8   http://www.nytimes.com/2014/02/24/us/politics/pentagon-plans-to-shrink-army-to-pre-world-war-ii-level.html

9   http://www.military.com/daily-news/2015/02/02/army-shrinks-force-by-23k-soldiers-in-2016-budget-proposal.html

10   http://www.pgpf.org/chart-archive/0053_defense-comparison

11   http://www.wsj.com/articles/u-s-general-says-strike-on-afghanistan-hospital-was-a-mistake-1444145615

12   Ibid.

13   http://www.theguardian.com/commentisfree/2011/oct/26/libya-war-saving-lives-catastrophic-failure

14   http://belfercenter.ksg.harvard.edu/publication/23387/lessons_from_libya.html

15   http://www.nytimes.com/2016/01/29/world/middleeast/more-is-needed-to-beat-isis-us-military-concludes.html

16   http://www.brookings.edu/research/articles/1998/12/balkans-daalder

17   http://fpif.org/women_of_bosnia_and_herzegovina_twenty_years_later/

18   https://history.state.gov/milestones/1993-2000/bosnia

19   https://open.buffer.com/sorry/

20   https://www.congress.gov/bill/114th-congress/senate-bill/2230/text

21   http://www.nationalreview.com/article/413310/roots-obamas-appeasement-victor-davis-hanson

22   https://www.armscontrol.org/factsheets/agreedframework

23   http://www.nytimes.com/interactive/2015/03/31/world/middleeast/simple-guide-nuclear-talks-iran-us.html

24   http://www.nytimes.com/2015/04/11/opinion/north-koreas-real-lessons-for-iran.html

25   http://www.telegraph.co.uk/finance/newsbysector/energy/oilandgas/11014604/Vladimir-Putin-signs-historic-20bn-oil-deal-with-Iran-to-bypass-Western-sanctions.html

26   http://moneymorning.com/2015/11/19/this-budding-russia-iran-oil-deal-would-open-the-door-to-asia/

27   http://www.cnn.com/2016/02/14/middleeast/syria-russia-u-s-turkey/

28   http://www.clarionproject.org/analysis/us-appeasement-iran-cuba-n-korea-shows-terror-works

29   http://foreignpolicy.com/2009/11/19/think-again-clintons-foreign-policy/?wp_login_redirect=0

30   http://www.cnbc.com/2015/10/12/chinas-military-and-naval-buildup-in-south-china-sea-threatens-the-us.html

31 http://theweek.com/articles/603994/americas-military-getting-deadly
    -serious-about-china-russia-north-korea
32 http://www.slate.com/articles/news_and_politics/politics/2015/11/military
    _spending_the_case_for_spending_more_not_less.single.html
33 Ibid.
34 Center for Strategic and Budgetary Assessments. *Assessment of the FY 2015
    Defense Budget*. By Todd Harrison. Washington, DC: Center for Strategic and
    Budgetary Assessments, 2014.
35 Ibid.
36 http://www.businessinsider.com/military-spending-budget-defense-cuts
    -2011-10
37 Center for Strategic and Budgetary Assessments. *Assessment of the FY 2015
    Defense Budget*. By Todd Harrison. Washington, DC: Center for Strategic and
    Budgetary Assessments, 2014.
38 http://www.bls.gov/ooh/military/mobile/military-careers.htm
39 http://historyinpieces.com/research/us-military-personnel-1954-2014
40 http://www.reuters.com/article/us-usa-military-officers-idUSN14325
    57920070514
41 http://www.theatlantic.com/politics/archive/2015/11/us-military-tries-halt
    -brain-drain/413965/
42 http://www.reuters.com/article/us-usa-pentagon-waste-specialreport
    -idUSBRE9AH0LQ20131118
43 http://thehill.com/policy/defense/budget-appropriations/237044-mccain
    -vows-to-fight-sequestration-wasteful-defense
44 http://www.thefiscaltimes.com/Articles/2014/04/09/45-Billion-Wasted
    -Redundant-Federal-Programs-GAO
45 http://www.heritage.org/research/reports/2009/10/50-examples-of
    -government-waste#_edn29
46 Ibid.
47 http://warontherocks.com/2015/10/is-u-s-intelligence-analysis-as-good
    -as-it-gets/
48 http://www.bga-aeroweb.com/Defense-Spending.html
49 http://www.businessinsider.com/how-the-us-military-spends-its
    -billions-2015-8
50 http://www.darpa.mil/about-us/budget
51 http://www.cfr.org/defense-budget/trends-us-military-spending/p28855
52 http://www.wired.com/2012/02/darpa-budget-death-ray/
53 http://thehill.com/policy/cybersecurity/242235-house-passed-defense
    -budget-fully-funds-cyber
54 http://time.com/3928086/these-5-facts-explain-the-threat-of-cyber-warfare/
55 http://www.wired.com/2014/11/countdown-to-zero-day-stuxnet/

56 http://www.heritage.org/research/reports/2010/11/emp-attacks-what-the-us-must-do-now
57 http://denisecua.tumblr.com/post/34471081481/it-is-with-passion-courage-of-conviction-and
58 http://www.hstoday.us/focused-topics/border-security/single-article-page/10-years-after-911/73541b6c516c10cc5dce5f91fee4c254.html

CHAPTER 7

1 https://blog.udemy.com/impact-of-globalization/
2 http://www.history.com/this-day-in-history/congress-issues-continental-currency
3 http://www.state.gov/r/pa/ei/bgn/3842.htm
4 https://www.loc.gov/rr/program/bib/ourdocs/alliance.html
5 http://www.earlyamerica.com/milestone-events/proclamation-neutrality/
6 http://www.u-s-history.com/pages/h453.html
7 http://www.businessinsider.com/heres-how-much-america-really-spends-on-israels-defense-2012-9
8 http://www.pewglobal.org/2015/06/23/1-americas-global-image/
9 http://www.state.gov/r/pa/ei/bgn/3581.htm
10 Ibid.
11 https://ustr.gov/countries-regions/europe-middle-east/middle-east/north-africa/israel
12 http://www.state.gov/r/pa/ei/bgn/3581.htm
13 Ibid.
14 Ronald Inglehart, "Inequality and Modernization," *Foreign Affairs*, January/February 2016, p. 2
15 Stephen Radlet, "Prosperity Rising," *Foreign Affairs*, January/February 2016, p. 86
16 https://library.cqpress.com/cqalmanac/document.php?id=cqal97-0000181071
17 Ibid.
18 http://foreignpolicy.com/2009/11/19/think-again-clintons-foreign-policy/
19 "The Summiteers Go to School," *The Economist*, April 25, 1998, p. 37.
20 http://www.heritage.org/research/reports/1998/07/clintons-latin-america-policy
21 http://www.theglobalist.com/latin-americas-corruption-crisis/
22 http://borgenproject.org/does-globalization-help-or-hurt-women/
23 http://www.huffingtonpost.com/2014/01/23/gender-inequality-latin-america_n_4653710.html
24 http://warontherocks.com/2014/07/terrorism-in-latin-america-infographic/

25 http://www.centerforsecuritypolicy.org/2015/01/17/in-latin-america-radical
    -islamic-presence-flourishes-while-key-countries-downplay-the-threat/
26 http://fortune.com/2015/10/13/free-trade-democrats/
27 http://dailysignal.com/2011/04/13/is-the-democratic-blockade-of-trade
    -really-over/
28 http://www.huffingtonpost.com/dave-johnson/now-we-know-why-huge
    -tpp_b_6956540.html
29 http://www.wipo.int/women-and-ip/en/
30 http://www.wipo.int/ipadvantage/en/details.jsp?id=2915
31 http://www.entrepreneur.com/article/227163
32 http://www.tampabay.com/topics/specials/worst-charities1.page
33 http://www.theglobalfund.org/en/government/
34 http://www.pepfar.gov/documents/organization/93712.pdf
35 http://www.un.org/press/en/2001/gbcpc.doc.htm
36 http://reliefweb.int/report/world/africa-big-business-takes-hivaids-challenge
37 http://archive.fortune.com/magazines/fortune/fortune_archive/2004/09
    /06/380315/index.htm
38 http://abcnews.go.com/blogs/politics/2013/04/george-w-bushs-legacy-on
    -africa-wins-praise-even-from-foes/
39 http://www.pepfar.gov/funding/results/index.htm
40 http://www.aidspan.org/gfo_article/sustainability-about-more-just-money
    -study-says
41 http://abcnews.go.com/blogs/politics/2013/04/george-w-bushs-legacy-on
    -africa-wins-praise-even-from-foes/
42 http://www.frbsf.org/economic-research/publications/economic-letter
    /2004/may/globalization-threat-or-opportunity-for-the-us-economy/
43 http://borgenproject.org/does-globalization-help-or-hurt-women/
44 http://www.wsj.com/articles/the-myths-of-chinas-currency-manipulation
    -1452296887
45 https://ourfuture.org/20150812/what-chinas-currency-devaluation-means
46 https://www.washingtonpost.com/lifestyle/style/miss-manners-public
    -plea-for-donations-may-be-politely-declined/2015/02/13/449614c4-b303
    -11e4-886b-c22184f27c35_story.html
47 http://www.pepfar.gov/about/strategy/document/133251.htm
48 Ibid.
49 http://borgenproject.org/lessons-learned-successes-pepfar/
50 https://www.wto.org/english/tratop_e/devel_e/a4t_e/a4t_factsheet_e.htm
51 http://www.oecd.org/trade/OECD-WTO-AFT-10-years-on.pdf
52 http://www.imf.org/external/pubs/ft/fandd/2012/03/revenga.htm
53 Steven Radlet, "Prosperity Rising," *Foreign Affairs*, January/February 2016,
    p. 95

EPILOGUE

1 http://www.pewsocialtrends.org/2012/04/19/a-gender-reversal-on-career
   -aspirations/
2 Ibid.
3 Ibid.